2261   1800

Women of the Range

Women o

WOMEN'S ROLES IN THE T

COLLEGE STATION

he Range

BEEF CATTLE INDUSTRY

Elizabeth Maret

Foreword by Liz Carpenter

TEXAS A&M UNIVERSITY PRESS

The paper used in this book meets the minimum requirements
of the American National Standard for Permanence
of Paper for Printed Library Materials, Z39.48–1984.
Binding materials have been chosen for durability.

LIBRARY OF CONGRESS CATALOGING-IN-PUBLICATION DATA

Maret, Elizabeth.
    Women of the range : women's roles in the Texas beef
cattle industry / Elizabeth Maret ; foreword by Liz Carpenter.
        p.   cm.
    Includes bibliographical references and index.
    ISBN 0-89096-532-3 (cloth). – ISBN 0-89096-541-2 (pbk.)
    1. Women in the cattle industry–Texas.   2. Women
ranchers–Texas.   3. Ranch life–Texas.   I. Title.
HD9433.U5T42   1993
331.4'836213'09764–dc20   92-45787
                                                                CIP

To Elizabeth Clark Maret

Contents

Illustrations

Foreword

Range women are strong, sturdy, delightful types. They've always had to struggle against the unknown—changing weather, changing economies, not to mention loneliness—the common traits of remote living. They take justifiable pride in meeting every challenge.

I like the story of Molly Goodnight, alone for weeks at a time on the famous J A Ranch in the Palo Duro Canyon back in the 1870s. She looked forward to having cowboys stop by, and when they did, she cooked dinner for them. One brought her several live chickens as a gift, to use as she needed them.

She kept them as pets and wrote her sister, "You've no idea how much company a chicken can be."

My mother and my grandmothers were ranch women. There was nothing they couldn't do and didn't have to do.

On a ranch in Uvalde Canyon in 1912–14, my mother, Mary Elizabeth Robertson Sutherland, overcame loneliness by writing poetry and by quoting the British poets to her small son, who remembered the lines of Byron, Shelley, and Keats to his death.

Then, there was a very wealthy ranch woman who once told me: "My front gate was seventy miles from the house and the only other person around was a Mexican ranch hand who spoke no English. So once a year I checked myself into an expensive spa—just for the conversation."

At a women's liberation gathering, I met a ranch woman, charming in her elegant haute couture ensemble. "You don't know what women's lib is," she said to me, smiling, "until you've lifted a 200-pound heifer calf into the back of a pickup truck by yourself." I agreed.

Today's women in ranching or related roles in the beef cattle industry face new challenges: computerization, breed and herd improvement, redesign of the product to suit changing dietary needs — not to mention women's evolving position of leadership in politics, the professions, and business.

In *Women of the Range*, Elizabeth Maret has given us an objective overview of a subject too long neglected.

Liz Carpenter

Preface

Ten years ago, I was introduced to the writings of a prominent Texas author, Larry McMurtry. In several of his "Essays on Texas" from *In a Narrow Grave* (1968), the image of women aroused my curiosity and my skepticism. According to McMurtry, "There just weren't that many women west of the Mississippi, and what there were tended to be work-worn and a discouraging distance apart" (1968, 56). Could women be as infrequent in and unimportant to the state of Texas as McMurtry suggested? Did women not make contributions to the history and economy of Texas as they did elsewhere? Attempts to answer this rather simple question were found to have many ramifications. Understanding Texas means understanding agriculture, in particular the beef cattle industry.

The cattle industry is the largest segment of the Texas agricultural economy. It is also imbedded in, and to some extent reflects, a historical and cultural myth. More than other agricultural work, the occupation of cattle rancher has been romanticized. The image of the rancher is a part of the mystique of the West—strongwilled, independent people making a living by working with cattle and horses and by overcoming the laws of nature and outwitting the principles of economics. As a child growing up in the fifties, I was also captivated by the myth of the rancher and the "cowboy." And the cowboys and ranchers I grew up with from the Roy Rogers and Dale Evans show and from the novels of Zane Gray and Emerson Hough were sometimes women. But women did not seem to count for much in the modern myths of McMurtry's Texas:

> I would not wish to make the point crudely, but I do find it possible to doubt that I have ever known a cowboy who liked women as well as he liked horses. . . . I did not believe this was the result of repressed homosexuality, but of a commitment to a heroic concept of life that simply takes little account of women.
> Commitment to the myth today carries with it a terrible emo-

tional price—very often the cowboy becomes a victim of his own ritual. His women, too, are victims, though for the most part acquiescent victims. They usually buy the myth of cowboying and the ideal of manhood it involves, even though both exclude them. A few even buy it to the point of attempting to assimilate the all-valuable masculine qualities to themselves, producing that awful phenomenon, the cowgirl. (1968, 147–48)

McMurtry's "heroic myth" might preclude cowgirls, but mine did not. As a social scientist, I could see no reason of nature or any universal law of society that would preclude the participation of women as cowgirls and ranchers. I did not think that horses would object to the fellowship of women. The social evidence I knew about suggested the possibility that women were more important to the reality of ranching than to the myth. Where there is agriculture, in particular family-based agriculture, there are women doing much of the work. Could ranching be different?

This was a question for research. What did the evidence show about the presence and contributions of Texas women? Here began my research to document the productive roles of Texas women. This research led me to many places. Beginning with the history of Texas, a graduate student and I studied census data from 1850 to 1880, expecting to find very few women, particularly in the frontier counties. We found women were there (chap. 2). I also found women who had written about their experiences on the frontier, and I found women in data published by the Texas Land Heritage Program. This program documents the origins of many Texas farms and ranches. Women were present in the early days of statehood (circa 1850), and they were there in numbers similar to men. Since Texas was and is highly dependent upon agricultural industries, I also wanted to address the question of women's productive roles in agriculture. Although the official record left a lot to be desired in the effort to identify the roles of women in agriculture, I found women to be present in agriculture in large numbers, especially in the status of unpaid family laborer and in the status of self-employment (chap. 2). A colleague and I published the results of this research in 1982. About this time the first and only national survey on farm and ranch women became available, allowing research on the actual contributions of farm and ranch women to the tasks and decisions made on family-run agricultural enterprises. Findings from this study were presented at the International Ranchers Roundup in San Angelo, Texas.

Conclusions are also included here (chap. 2). Women are present on farms and ranches in large numbers and in myriad roles.

Now time had come to focus more narrowly on Texas women. I decided to look at the romanticized and male-identified occupation of rancher. Before I discovered the Texas Land Heritage Program, the going had been slow, as I had not identified any other systematic source of information. However, once the identification process began, I was overwhelmed with the names of ranching women, many of whom owned and managed their own ranches. At this point the research took a turn toward the qualitative. Numbers were simply not sufficient to describe the experiences and feelings of the ranching women I came to know.

I started my study as a highly quantitative venture based on government data. However, the shortcomings of official data soon became apparent. This led me to less official sources and ultimately to my own observations gained from intensive interviews of ranching women and a five-year participant observation of women in the cattle industry. During that period I helped run a purebred cattle business, received certification as an AI (artificial insemination) technician, became a licensed auctioneer, and developed abiding affection and respect for the subjects I came to know—the women of the Texas range. I am grateful to all the wonderful people who were part of this research.

I am also grateful for the support of Lloyd Lyman, former director of Texas A&M University Press, and for the input of Dr. Ruth Schaffer, colleague and friend, whose light illuminated the end of the tunnel.

Elizabeth Maret

Introduction

The goal of this study is first and foremost descriptive – to describe women's presence and roles in what many consider to be a masculine industry. Are women represented in the Texas beef cattle industry and in what ways are they represented?

The Questions

The major questions for investigation are from an area of sociology termed "women and work," in particular, (1) what positions or statuses do women occupy in the beef cattle industry, and (2) what roles as workers and managers do women perform? At first these questions focused only on women ranchers, but I soon learned that there are many important occupations held by women in the modern beef cattle industry. Indeed, industry-related occupational roles for women seem to be expanding with advances in technology. This led to a second research focus, discovered in the process of answering the first questions about women's work as ranchers.[1] The beef cattle industry is undergoing radical and rapid technological change. From the area of research termed women in development (or WID) the following question is important: What happens to women's productive roles in the process of technological change or development? Are their roles reduced with increased capitalization and technology?

Questions about women and work and women in development relate to central questions of women's studies regarding women's visibility and contributions. In their conference report "Women and Farming" (1987), Wava Haney and Jane Knowles state that there is a "common concern of particular urgency." The urgency is for greater visibility for women's agricultural roles and "recognition of the enormous economic contribution women make to agricultural systems in every country of the world" (Haney and Knowles 1987, 800). Finally, from feminist research comes the question of the experiences and feelings of women themselves. Often overlooked in research on women (and men) is the qualitative question of what women *feel* who are part of a particular industry. What is the quality of their experience? In many ways this is the most difficult of the questions to answer. It is difficult because of the diversity of women's roles, and it is difficult adequately to portray feelings. Sometimes, also, it is difficult to separate one's own feelings toward the subjects from what the subjects are feeling. The re-creation of meaning and *verstehen* (understanding) is, in some ways, a greater challenge than the requirements of quantitative analysis. Nevertheless, I have tried to include findings from diverse quantitative and qualitative research materials that best address questions of the status and roles of women in the economically important and changing beef cattle industry.

Data and Methods

This book is based on a combination of quantitative and qualitative data. The types of data correspond roughly to three research stages and three types of observations. The data are drawn from the analysis of government census statistics, survey research, and participant observation.

Analysis of government census data is a highly quantitative venture. The data are aggregate, and little is known or can be derived about the experiences of individuals. For example, the historical census data provided in chapter 2 are used to present a "demographic profile" of women's representation by county. We do know something about the counties, in particular that women were present in almost all Texas counties existing at the time of statehood, but we know nothing about the lives of individual women. The aggregated census data are valid for some purposes, but they are very limited. The sources of census data from the U.S. Bureau of the Census and the U.S. Department of Agriculture (USDA) (agricultural and livestock censuses) are given with the text in which they are discussed.

For information on the experiences of individuals, survey data are a better source. Survey research is also very versatile. It allows for highly structured information that lends itself to quantitative interpretations, and it can also be used to gather rather unstructured "qualitative" data. In the latter case, a less structured interview guide is substituted for the more highly structured interview schedule or the mailed questionnaire.

Over the years, there had been only small survey studies of farm women (small in terms of numbers and geographic scope) until in 1979 the U.S. Department of Agriculture allocated funds for a nationwide survey of farm women. The survey of 2,509 farm women and 569 men (mostly husbands of female respondents) was undertaken by the National Opinion Research Center (NORC) in cooperation with the USDA. In this survey, a "farm woman" is defined as the farm or ranch operator or the wife of the operator (even if widowed, divorced, or separated). To be eligible for this survey, respondents had to be operating farms, ranches, or other agricultural businesses in 1980. One of the objectives of the study was to collect basic information from a representative sample of farm women about their involvement in the work tasks and management decisions of their operations. Initial findings were published in 1981 (Jones and Rosenfeld 1981). My project uses data from the USDA-NORC survey.

This project also uses survey data obtained by the Texas Family Land Heritage Program from mailed questionnaires. The Land Heritage Program represents an effort to document the history of Texas farms and ranches which have been in continuous production and owned by the same family for one hundred years or more. As of 1984, approximately 1,680 heritage properties had been identified.

Both of these sources of survey information represent secondary analyses of survey data gathered by other organizations for purposes other than this study of ranching women. Specific, detailed and more qualitative data on Texas ranch women were obtained from personal interviews of ranch owners and operators conducted between the spring of 1984 and the winter of 1986. During this time I interviewed women ranchers near Kurten (Brazos County), Gatesville (Coryell County), Marfa (Presidio County), Alpine (Brewster County), and Bay City (Matagorda County). The ranches were distributed across three major natural regions of the state.

I originally intended to interview women in each of ten topographical and climatic subregions (Pool 1975, 6–12). The decision to limit the interviews reflects several considerations: (1) ranches are not evenly distributed throughout the geographic subregions; (2) the large number of women ranchers in subregions close to home, coupled with the paucity of time and funds for travel, made these areas better interview targets; and (3) the discovery of many more occupations in which women are represented within the modernizing cattle industry made me eager to pursue this direction of research. Limitations of time and money as well as serendipitous findings can and do influence research directions.

Each interview lasted approximately three to four hours, with additional time for touring the ranches (in one case, the interview spanned two days. I went back and revisited the respondent after revising the interview guide). A loosely structured interview schedule was used for the interviews (see appendix). I used a tape recorder during the interviews and took photographs to assist in the recollection and presentation of information.

It was during this phase of research that I began to use and rely on the tape recorder as a field research tool. In addition to its use to record interviews, I used to it record notes, impressions, and even ideas and feelings I had about the ongoing research process. My small microrecorder was an unobtrusive and reliable research tool, indispensable to me when I did not have access to a typewriter or computer or could not stop to write notes, for example, while driving. There were some problems with transcribing the oral to the written—it requires a fast typist to keep up with the spoken word. Nevertheless, the tape recorder was an important and sometimes essential field research tool. At the very least, it augmented memory and complemented both the interview guide and written field notes. At most it was an accurate confidant, unerringly recalling intonations and feelings of the field experience.

The tape recorder is a most unobtrusive and compliant tool. Photographs, on the other hand, require both interruption and intention. However, I decided to take photographs because they do add a dimension to the written (or even oral) record. Sometimes a photograph will depict a quality that words do not capture. I feel some of the photographs taken during the course of interviewing and field work make such a contribution. Some of the best photographs were taken by my husband, Sam, who has completed courses in photographic techniques. On my own as I often was, I simply got lucky, working with a camera that knew more than I did about photographs.[2]

Initially, I identified ranch women from responses to announcements that I placed in the agricultural sections of newspapers and in agriculture-related seminars.[3] Once the interviewing process had begun, many more names were provided by the respondents (this is a technique called "snowballing"). I located additional respondents by visiting county fairs (obtaining names of those showing cattle) and cattle sales (obtaining names of those selling or buying cattle), by obtaining membership lists of the various breed associations (see the directories listed in the reference list), and by identifying women through advertisements and articles in the various trade publications (such as the *Cattleman,* published by the Texas and Southwestern Cattle Raisers Association). In this way I also discovered women in many of the auxiliary occupations.

My usual procedure was to follow up the more promising recommendations and "leads" on ranching women with a letter of introduction (in several cases with women in the auxiliary occupations, I simply called to introduce myself). In most cases my introductory letters were answered, and on the basis of the response, I would decide to arrange an interview or simply to settle for correspondence. I obtained a list of forty-one names from referrals. Another twenty-five to thirty names of women owners and operators (there was some overlap) were obtained from the trade publications and membership listings and from personal observations (at cattle sales, shows, seminars). From this list I chose twelve to interview on the basis of three criteria: (1) the women had to own and manage the ranch; (2) the selected ranches had to represent the size distribution of Texas ranches (that is, they must represent both the predominant small and middle-sized ranches as well as the "romanticized" large ranches); and (3) the selected ranches should represent the geographic distribution of Texas ranches. Two of the names I chose did not respond to my request for an interview. I actually undertook eight interviews of cow-calf ranchers. Five of those interviews are reported here as personal profiles in chapter 3. These five profiles selected for chapter 3 are all of commercial cow-calf operators, which provides a commonality. There is a second commonality among the five ranchers profiled in chapter 3: they are all women who own and manage their ranches. The other interviews, of purebred breeders, are used to provide illustrative materials in other chapters. In the process of interviewing women ranchers, I discovered that many, indeed most, of the purebred breeders had occupations in addition to ranching. Some of these occupations were part of what I came to see as an expanding base of occupational opportunities for women in the beef cattle industry brought about by technological and social change. In some ways the women ranchers represented the tip of the iceberg of women's productive roles in the beef cattle industry.

In part because of the complexities of structure and change within the industry, and because I wanted to learn as much as possible in a short period, I entered the industry as a participant observer in the spring of 1985.

This participant observation characterized the third stage of my research. In 1985 I formed my own cattle company and joined the purebred sector of the beef cattle industry as a participant observer. Sometimes traveling with husband and son and often going alone, I attended dozens of cattle sales, including purebred and commercial, and met hundreds of women, men, and young people associated with the industry. It was during this phase that I identified and subsequently interviewed most of the women in the auxiliary or supporting occupations. I conducted the first of these interviews by telephone during the final phases of the rancher interviews, but most of the interviews of women in the auxiliary occupations were face-to-face. I conducted the last of the personal interviews in January, 1989.

All my observations of the women in auxiliary occupations had a direct participant component that sometimes spanned several years. For example, I first observed Heddy Butler (computer programmer) at a purebred cattle sale in South Texas in the fall of 1986. I interviewed her at the dispersion of that same ranch in January, 1989.[4] In the meantime I identified many of her customers and learned about her programs so that when the time came for the interview I already knew quite a lot about her business. Each of the observations of the women reported in chapter 4 includes information gathered over a period of time rather than at a single point. Each also includes information I gained through at least one interview, if only by phone. As an example, I observed Cindy Warnke, cattle fitter, at many shows over a three-year period and also visited her facilities near Castroville. I interviewed over the phone about halfway through the observation process. I used an interview guide in each of these interviews, but each guide was highly individualized. Unlike the guide for the ranching women, which could be used for all with only minor variations as experience enlightened the interviews, each of the women in chapter 4 pursued a different occupation and required a unique set of questions. Indeed, the interview did not always conclude the observation. Although I have not revisited any of the ranching women since their interviews, I have continued to meet and observe some of the women in chapter 4, particularly through the spring of 1989. My participation in the cattle industry has been much more limited since I concluded my research plan in the spring of 1989, but I continue to follow the industry with considerable interest.

Organization of the Book

Having begun with analysis of census data in the early 1980s, the process of research spanned almost a decade. The different modes of observation correspond somewhat to the development of the research and the organization of the book.

The beginning stages of investigation, represented by the broad background material in chapter 1, began the search for women's contributions to agricultural enterprises through the analysis of government statistics, primarily U.S. census data and data from the census of agriculture. Until 1981 these aggregated census data were the best data available on the economic contributions of farm and ranch women, and much of the information was inferential (Maret and Copp 1982). In 1981 Jones and Rosenfeld published the results of the first national survey on farm and ranch women, and the data became available to me in 1983. Included in the survey was information on women's contributions to farm and ranch tasks and decisions. Some of these findings are also presented in chapter 1. The analysis of these national survey data and the decision to survey ranch women in Texas represent the beginning of the second phase of the research.

The survey research phase of the project lasted for approximately three years, from 1983 to 1986. During this time, I analyzed data on ranching women from the USDA–NORC tape, spent time in Austin looking at data from the Texas Department of Agriculture Family Land Heritage Program, looked over the archives of the Texas and Southwestern Cattle Raisers Association in Fort Worth, Texas, visited the Cowgirl Hall of Fame in Hereford, Texas, and undertook the field interviews of ranching women. This research focused on the presence and productive contributions of women ranchers. Information from this research phase is reported in chapters 2 and 3. Chapter 2 focuses on ranching women of the past. Chapter 3 looks at contemporary ranching women.

Chapter 4 reports the participant observation phase of the research. The material in this chapter on auxiliary occupations is divided roughly into three sections: herd health, information technology, and the cattle associations. There is, of course, some overlap among these dimensions of the modernizing beef cattle industry. Chapter 5 draws together all the research streams, offers some conclusions about the past and present roles of women, and makes some cautious predictions about the future of women's status and roles in the Texas beef cattle industry of the year 2000 and beyond.

Women of the Range

1

Women and Ranching

PAST, PRESENT, AND FUTURE

Over a century ago the Texas cattle industry emerged out of the wilderness of colonial Texas with trail drives to supply the East with beef. According to Walter P. Webb (1931), the cattle kingdom began when men on horseback began to manage cattle. Although the drives to eastern markets were irregular and relatively restricted prior to 1860, after the Civil War the cattle kingdom expanded when "Texans discovered that a range cow worth three to four dollars in Texas would bring thirty to forty dollars on the northern market" (Pool 1975, 120). Basically, the economic goal of people in the beef cattle industry is still to buy or raise cattle at a low price and sell them at a later time (or distance) for a high price. As one of Texas's most prominent auctioneers once told me, "You don't make money when you sell cattle but when you buy them" (Col. Walter Britten, Britten Auction Seminar, June, 1987).

The margin of profit between buying and selling or raising and selling cattle is the economic "bottom line" in the beef cattle industry. This bottom line depends on many interrelated factors, including the interplay between supply and demand, the cost of feed and supplies, the health of the cattle, and always the weather. Luck plays a considerable part in making money on cows today, as it did over a century ago. The late 1870s represented a "golden era" for the range cattle industry (Pool 1975, 122). The era passed with the coming of barbed wire, which also signaled the end of the open cattle trails. Although the great cattle drives of the post–Civil War era were of fairly short duration in the development of the cattle industry, the drives became an important part of cultural history. Many people still think of that era as the apex of the industry, although the cattle business continued to grow well beyond the open range and cattle drive stage.

There is no doubt that the structure of the beef cattle industry has changed from the time of the cattle trails to the present. Indeed, the structure of society has changed markedly. No longer do most people make their living from the land. No longer is most of the population employed in agriculture. No longer is the population predominantly rural or dispersed. No longer are families large and labor cheap. No longer is government land for grazing extensive and unfenced. No longer is land purchase inexpensive. No longer are taxes unconstitutional. Large ranches with low stocking rates (number of cows per acre) and with long distances to haul cattle to markets are not profitable or even feasible in the ecological, economic, and social world of the late twentieth century. In Texas cattle sales are dispersed in more than 150 state-inspected commercial auction barns located around the state. The drives to these auction markets, usually by truck and trailer, are expensive in terms of stress on the cows as well as the cost rate per mile. Opportunities to be ranchers in the old style—rounding up and rodeoing large numbers of wild cows in wild country and moving them by horseback to markets or pens—are increasingly rare. Very few ranches in Texas continue to operate in the stereotypical tradition, where labor and land are cheap, where equipment consists of a good horse and a good rope (try dehorning a cow without a head chute), and where markets are concentrated and hugely profitable. Even old-time ranches are likely to use modern techniques of palpation (pregnancy testing), record keeping, and herd health maintenance. Unless they do, they are not likely to remain in the business of raising and selling cattle.

Ranching requires resources of knowledge and experience, and it requires money. There are very few ranches left in the state of Texas, or elsewhere in the United States, that survive without income from other sources. The most traditional ranching operations often rely on income from oil or gas leases, hunting leases, and other ventures, and the majority also rely on off-farm income. The costs of land, equipment, maintenance, taxes, feed, labor, and cows are simply too high and the cattle markets too precarious to make ranching a good choice as an occupation, even when that choice is available. Ranching is no longer the sole or even the predominant occupation for most ranchers. Ranchers are teachers, lawyers, physicians, extension specialists, contractors, small business owners. They are people who can afford to have and maintain ranches.

There is consensus within the industry that the trend is toward the more economically efficient larger units of several hundred head. Such units are able to produce the more uniform calf crops desired by the buyers. These larger units are often able to "background" or support animals all the way to slaughter or even to market. There is some evidence suggesting that vertical integration is increasingly important to the success of beef cattle producers. The little producer finds it difficult to compete with the large, capital-intensive operator who owns the feedlot, retail outlets, and restaurants which offer the producer's "branded beef." Branded beef, which can command a premium price, is not usually the product of the small operator.

Today, most cattle producers are not totally dependent upon their cows for income. In the past (and, perhaps in the future), monies from oil leases and real estate have bought and supported many a cow. These revenues have been supplemented by hunting leases and for some (especially the larger ranchers) by generous lines of bank credit. However, with the exception of hunting rights, these sources of revenue disappeared in the 1980s. Oil money was gone, real estate money was gone, and many of the banks were gone. Even the tax advantages of investment credit and accelerated depreciation were gone. For a two-year period during the 1980s, the producer could not even deduct the expenses of raising replacement heifers. The so-called "heifer tax" has now been repealed. However, many of the economic advantages of cattle production, such as the robust tax deductions, remain a thing of the past.

These economic changes are taking place at a time when beef is commanding a lower share of the food market. In 1976 beef had a 48 percent share of the total meat market. In 1985 this share had dropped to 37 percent. The beef cattle industry has responded to the health concerns and demands of consumers in two ways. First, there is a new awareness and emphasis on consumer education about the nutritional properties of beef. Second, there is a new emphasis on producing a lean beef animal. These efforts to "genetically engineer" a leaner product require extensive information about both inheritance and performance values and, once more, meticulous records.

Besides money, ranching requires much knowledge: knowledge of genetics, health, cow physiology and psychology, flood control, fire prevention, soils, grasses and grains, nutrition, reproduction, markets, fencing. Welding comes in handy, as does a working knowledge of tractor and truck mechanics. Palpation and certification in artificial insemination (AI) are also survival tools for the competitive cow-calf producer. Being raised on a ranch or, at least around cows, is a good start. Otherwise, the aspiring rancher should be prepared to become proficient in all the areas mentioned above plus a few others—for example, how to get water to cows when the tanks are frozen (as Ethel Williams does in chapter 3), how to swim cows across a flooded river (as Martha Ann Clements Lawhorn knows), or how to treat a rattlesnake bite or to get yourself off of the horns of an angry mother cow (as Angela Bonifazi has done). Knowledge of the computer is an increasingly important tool for keeping track of cattle (Maurine Godbolt). And the rancher should be prepared to travel hundreds of miles to find the best bulls for her program, to bargain for the best price, and to keep abreast of the most progressive herd management techniques (Jackie Worthington). Finally, the rancher must be prepared to do all of this, when need be, unassisted, alone.

The occupation of rancher has changed markedly in the last 150 years—much of the change occurring in the past twenty-five years. The changes associated with ranching have also been associated with the growth of auxiliary occupations in the ranching industry, many of which serve to support the rancher.

Although ranching has long been noted as an independent occupation for self-reliant people, increasingly ranchers must depend upon agricultural service industries to survive. This is true for the maintenance of herd health and reproductive efficiency, for herd marketing and sales, for herd performance, and for purebred breeders, the show ring. All of these areas have seen the appearance of new occupations, such as performance records specialists, and the expansion of old occupations, such as veterinary medicine. In addition to occupations that have grown up around the actual production of beef, there are occupations that have come into being, or at least come into prominence, in the beef cattle industry in association with the intersection between beef production and beef consumption. There is a new awareness and emphasis on the needs and preferences of the consumer. These preferences are measured by the application of social science techniques. Surveys to determine the preferences of conumers and to measure consumer response to various educational programs have become a popular tool of the beef producer trade associations and of the new Beef Checkoff Program inaugurated and supported by beef producers. Furthermore, the nutritionist is the new public relations star of the cattle industry. Research is being supported at both Texas A&M and the University of Texas to seek new evidence about the type of fat consumed in beef. The contemporary cattle industry is served by many occupations to improve, support, and promote its products.

The Texas Beef Cattle Industry

The "golden age" of the cattle drive began in 1867 when major cattle trails extended from South Texas to the Red River and then northeasterly along the Shawnee Trail, or Texas Road to destinations like Fort Gibson, Baxter Springs, and Sedalia.[1] Having begun in the southern tip of Texas, the cattle industry spread north and west into the Texas Panhandle and the northwestern plains. Indeed, the history of Texas is often phrased in terms of the development of the cattle industry. The early years of settlement coincide with the development of this enterprise (Pool 1975, 120–35).

Since the early days of statehood the livestock industry "has been a major economic boon to Texas" (Texas Department of Agriculture 1985). Don Worcester writes:

> The 1850s were profitable years for Texas cowmen who trailed herds to Missouri, Illinois, Louisiana, and California. Those driven north followed the route that came to be known as the Shawnee Trail, past Austin, Waco, and Dallas, crossing the Red River near Preston. Some herds were sold at Saint Louis, but others crossed eastern Kansas to Independence or Kansas City. (1987, 41)

A century and a half later the Texas cattle industry remains the leading agricultural industry of the state, and the image of a Texan, particularly for people who live in other states, is often synonymous with the image of the cattle rancher. The identification of Texas with the cattle industry is strong and not altogether incorrect. The cattle industry continues to be a dominant force in the economy and society of Texas.

The cattle industry is the single largest component of the Texas agricultural economy, and beef cattle make up the largest segment of the industry. According to the 1988–1989 *Texas Almanac* (1987, 582–83) the following characteristics are descriptive of the beef

cattle industry in Texas: (1) Beef cattle raising is the most extensive agricultural operation in Texas. In 1985, 44 percent of the
total receipts from farm and ranch marketing – $4,103,598,000 of
$9,262,549,000 – came from cattle and calves; (2) Nearly all of the
254 counties in Texas derive more revenue from cattle than from
any other agricultural commodity, and those that don't usually
rank cattle second; (3) Within the boundaries of Texas are 13 percent of all the cattle in the United States, as are 16 percent of
the beef breeding cows and 12 percent of the calf crop.

Texas has more beef cattle and more cattle ranches than any
state in the nation. Texas ranks first in the number of farms and
ranches, the number of cattle operations (152,000 in 1984),[2] the
value of farm real estate, value of cattle and calves, cattle on feed,
cattle slaughtered, calf crop, steers over five hundred pounds, beef
cows that have calved, and cash receipts for cattle and calves.[3]
The beef cattle industry in Texas is extensive. However, there is
considerable variation among beef cattle operations.

First, sizes of beef cattle operations vary in numbers of cattle
and in number of acres. The image of the Texas ranch is of a large,
labor-intensive operation employing numerous cowboys. In reality, the acreage of the operation depends upon the stocking rate,
meaning the number of cows per acre. In fertile areas of the state
the ranches do not need to be so large, because cows can be
"stocked" in higher concentrations, such as a cow per two or three
acres.[4] However, in the dry arid counties the stocking rate can
be as low as one cow per ten to twenty acres in a good year, as
is the case with the multiple-section West Texas ranches, which
are largely associated with the popular myths of ranching. Fortunately the ranching heritage of Texas is not dependent upon
these vast ranches, because when droughts do not decimate their
numbers, low cattle prices and land taxes do. These ranches have
a relatively low survival rate, and often their survival is more a
matter of the hunting and oil leases than the cattle raised on them.
Nevertheless, and against all odds of "man and nature," there are
women running and maintaining multigeneration and multisec-
tion ranches in West Texas; you will meet one such rancher in
chapter 3.

Despite the stereotype of the large cattle ranch, the majority
of Texas ranches have fewer than 100 cows. Indeed, the largest
percentage of cattle operations in Texas are relatively small.[5] Of
Texas cattle operations 84 percent have fewer than 100 cows (55

percent have 10 to 49 head), while approximately 9 percent of ranches have 100 to 199 head of cattle. Hence, 93 percent of Texas cattle ranchers have relatively small operations. Only 7 percent of cattle operations have 200 head or more.[6] Although the prototypical rancher owns fewer than 100 cows, changes taking place in the beef cattle industry would seem to favor the large producers. Much of the cattle inventory is accounted for by the large producers. Almost half of the beef cattle (42 percent) in Texas are owned by the 1.4 percent of operations having 500 head or more. The smaller producers account for a much smaller share of the cattle inventory. Only 27 percent of the inventory is held by operations of fewer than 100 cows, while 31 percent of the inventory is held by operations having 100 to 499 head. The economic climate or "the economy of scale" for the business of ranching would seem to favor the large producer of cattle as it favors large producers in other American industries, even the education industry. However, the industry of ranching is not just about business. Ranching is also about families and tradition and ways of life. These elements in the ranching equation make for a more diverse industry than could be understood on the basis of a single economic variable.

Not only do beef cattle ranches differ in land size and cattle numbers, beef cattle ranches also vary in type. The majority of Texas cattle operations are commercial "cow-calf" operations. These operations have mother cows ("the factories") which produce the bull and heifer calves to be sold. The bull calves are usually castrated into "steers" and sold on the commercial market. The heifer calves can be sold on the commercial market (they usually bring less than the steers) or retained as "replacement heifers" or future mother cows.

There are two types of cow-calf operations: commercial and purebred. The commercial, by far the most common cow-calf operation, is oriented toward producing a product to be marketed directly to the feedlot to be fattened for slaughter or sold to other operations to be fattened or "backgrounded" and then sold for slaughter. In Texas there are huge feedlots containing thousands of cattle being fattened in dry lots and destined for slaughter. These feedlots are concentrated in the Panhandle area near Amarillo.[7] The cattle ranches, where cows are bred and raised, continue to be dispersed throughout the state (although not evenly distributed).

When the calves are ready to be sold (usually around wean-

ing), they often are taken to local auction houses where they are
sold to buyers from the feedlots and packing houses. The commercial market for calves is based on a price per hundred pounds,
with the lighter weight calves bringing proportionally higher prices;
for example, calves under four hundred pounds can sell for $100
per "cwt" or per hundred pounds of weight, while calves over five
hundred pounds bring $80 to $85 per cwt. There are many variations on this theme. Ranchers can choose to feed out their own
calves or to vary the time of selling to maximize their profits, but
the intention of the commercial cow-calf operation is to sell calves
for beef. Eventually most beef cattle, even in the purebred sector,
go to the auction barn. Older cows are "culled" as their fertility
declines, and the bulls are also sold for slaughter. Prices for these
culls are not as high per pound, but the greater weight of these
older animals (a bull or large frame cow can weigh in excess of
fifteen hundred pounds) makes them attractive products, particularly when the market is high.

Another type of cow-calf operation is that of the breeder who
raises purebred bulls for the commercial rancher and seedstock
for other purebred breeders or, when the market is right, for the
commercial rancher who wants to use straightbred or F1 cows.[8]
These animals sell per individual or "head," rather than per pound,
although weight and age influence the sale prices. Many commercial ranchers like to use a straightbred mother cow. For example, in the Trans-Pecos area, it is difficult to find ranchers who
use other than straight Hereford cows, while commercial ranchers
in other parts of the state might use Hereford bulls on straight-
bred Angus cows. The object is to produce as much weight at
weaning with as little expense for feed and health costs as possible.

It is not uncommon to find cattle ranches, particularly the larger
operations, with both purebred and commercial components. This
is an ideal situation, for it maximizes the potential for outstand-
ing purebred individuals from a large genetic base and provides
an outlet for the lower performing purebreds which can be "down-
graded" into a commercial herd. The modern rancher, whether
a commercial or purebred producer, is likely to be interested in
performance.

Performance can be described as the ability of the individual
animal or herd to reach certain growth and beef characteristics.
For example, weaning weight is of tremendous importance both
to the commercial and purebred breeder. Both want to maximize

this performance characteristic. The commercial breeder wants as many pounds at weaning as possible because this will determine her success (profit) at the sale barn. The purebred breeder wants as many pounds at weaning as possible because weight is highly correlated with success (profit) at purebred sales and with success (winning) in the show ring. There are many performance characteristics, including maternal characteristics, which are projected by computer on the basis of information about related individuals. Most purebred breeders and many commercial breeders rely on these computer-generated characteristics, called EBVs (estimated breeding values) or EPVs (estimated performance values), to help select animals for their programs. There is a lot of record keeping in the modern cattle business. Increasingly, these records are computer-based.

Performance data are also used in the show ring. The show ring is both an important promotional tool for purebred breeders and a popular activity for youth. Youth in 4H, FFA, and the junior breed associations compete vigorously for the ribbons, trophies, and prizes in pride, that accompany the various contests. The show ring is not only for juniors. Many adults are serious competitors. A purebred animal that wins in the show ring is almost guaranteed to bring a bonus in the sale ring, as are his or her offspring. The show ring represents big money for the purebred breeder, and winning is serious business for members of ranching families including men, women, and children. In addition to increasing the value of livestock, valuable prizes and scholarships worth hundreds of thousands of dollars are given away annually in conjunction with the livestock shows.

The cattle industry is today, as it has been from the beginning, a family affair. The majority of Texas ranches are owned, managed, and worked by family members. Indeed, many Texas ranches have been in continuous production and owned by the same family for a hundred years or more (see data from the Texas Land Heritage Program in chapter 2). Certainly, the cattle industry has undergone radical transformation since the early days of statehood. One thing has not changed that dramatically: Ranching is usually a family business.

Although there are large, even multinational, corporations present in the cattle business, such as Granada Corporation (see chapter 4), most ranches are owned and worked by family members. Even Granada Corporation was owned and operated by two brothers before it went public in 1990. Ranching is still a family affair, and these families usually include women.

Women in Ranching

It ain't easy bein' a cowboy
like the Marlboro man.
'Cause the public expects us
to all be from Texas
And roll cigarettes in one hand.
>   Livestock Market Digest
>   (April 21, 1986)

Ranching is a particularly romanticized agricultural industry.[9] The myths surrounding ranching are part of a popular cultural heritage characterized by a peculiar absence or invisibility. With rare exception, women appear to be missing from the ranching heritage that is reflected in contemporary culture. To say that the image of women in Texas has been scantily and superficially drawn is to understate the situation. Given the particularly legendary character of the Texas cattle industry, women's part in this great and historic activity can most accurately be described as invisible.

The prototypical Texan is usually flamboyant, often violent, and always male. As Joe Frantz writes in his book *Texas: A Bicentennial History,* "Texans, much like the State itself, are 'flamboyant', 'violent', and 'bigger and tougher than life'" (quoted in Myres, 1985). According to Joseph Leach, "the typical Texan" emerged in the 1860s, "crystallized along the lines of 'the Wild Cowhand' and fellows like him" (also in Myres, 1985). Even today, writes Sandra Myres, "The image of the Texan that rises most often to the surface is this picture of the Typical Texan and Wild Cowhand" (1985, 16).

In his famous essays on West Texas, Larry McMurtry expresses a consistent and dominant theme in contemporary literary productions about the character of Texas—that women were few, far between, and "work-worn" (McMurtry 1968, 56).

Although McMurtry concedes that "the West isn't entirely a man's world anymore" (1968, 73), both the literary and historical images of the Texas cattle industry have been and continue to be narrowly defined: "the cattle kingdom arose at that place where *men* began to manage cattle on horseback" (Webb 1931, emphasis added). Beside the use of the horse, there is something else that distinguishes the Western cattle industry from Eastern stock-farming in the public imagination – something so commonly assumed that nomenclature presumes the specifics of gender.[10] Those who are involved in the industry, those who define the culture, are masculine.

Dorothy Smith explains the invisibility of women in the making of culture not as a deficiency in women but as a matter of male power and authorship:

> The universe of ideas, images and themes – the symbolic modes which are the general currency of thought – have been either produced by men or controlled by them. In so far as women's work and experience has been entered into it, it has been on terms decided by men and because it has been approved by men.
>
> The exclusion of women from the making of our culture is not the product of a biological deficiency or a biological configuration of some kind. As we learn more of our (women's) history we discover that a powerful intellectual and artistic current moves like an underground stream through the history of the last few centuries. (1989, 4, 7)

Although the image of the Western cattle industry is overwhelmingly male, there is a stream of work which contradicts the myth of a dominant male cattle culture.

Certainly, evidence about the status and roles of ranching women is limited compared with the extensive documentation about men. Published information about women in ranching tends to be historical and anecdotal. Among the best and most widely available of the historical chronicles are Sallie Matthews's *Interwoven* (1936), which tells the story of two Texas ranching families; Ada Holland's *Brush Country Woman* (1988), which is an excellent account of the life of Helen Sewell Harbison; and Mary Bunton's *A Bride on the Old Chisholm Trail* (1939). Cathy Luchetti's *Women of the West* (1982) provides "diverse stories" along with excellent photographs about "those women who have not had a place in academic history" (Luchetti 1982, 14). Similarly Teresa Jordan's *Cowgirls* presents an oral history of "women who work outside, on ranches or in the rodeo, on a regular basis" (1984, xxvi). Joyce Roach's *The Cowgirls* (1977) also presents reminiscences and impressions of women in the cattle business "from the frontier to the footlights" (1977, xix).

In different ways, all these writers call the myth of the masculine cattle industry into question. Three of them attack the myths directly. Roach feels there was considerable equality between women and men in the early days of the cattle industry. She writes that "it seems a pity that Susan B. Anthony did not live in the West where, once the cows the horses accepted you, the men generally followed suit. I am inclined to attach some importance to a theory that the emancipation of women may have begun when they mounted a good cowhorse and realized how different and fine the view was" (1977, xv).

Jordan emphasizes the personal characteristics of her women of the American West: "A cowgirl is not just a woman who lives on a ranch or hangs around the rodeo. She is the female counterpart of the cowboy. . . . If she does not embrace the land and the stock, she is not a cowgirl" (Jordan 1984, xxvi). Luchetti observes that history seldom tells the stories of the eight hundred thousand women who also came West. These women experienced an autonomy never before dreamed of, and with this new freedom came the necessity to solve their problems in any way they could: "Making do became an art shared by both sexes, and 'women's work' soon came to mean whatever had to be done, whether it was herding cattle, checking trap lines, or seeding the rows with corn" (Luchetti and Olwell 1982, 31).

There are wonderful and lively accounts of women associated with the cattle industry, particularly with ranching and rodeoing. There has, however, been little academic interest in ranching women. Perhaps the ranching industry is too male-identified to inspire the question and investigation of women's roles. Or, perhaps, the study of women in agriculture is too recent and too regional to have developed a literature for specific and western agricultural industries. Whatever the reason, most research, including recent government studies of women's agricultural roles, has focused on farm women.

Women's Agricultural Roles: The Existing Evidence

The official, government record is of limited value in correcting the myths surrounding the ranching industry. Indeed, it is likely that the official record is often informed by the myth. For example, the census of agriculture assumes that there is only one "main operator" on family-owned agricultural enterprises. It further assumes that this operator is a man unless there is no adult male present. The labor provided by other family members is relegated to the category of "unpaid family labor." Thus, women who own ranches with their husbands, or even married women who have inherited their ranches as separate property,[11] are often lost in the official tallies. Their ranches would be counted as male operated and even male owned.

In general, according to a report from the USDA, "The position of farm women remains a mystery" (Ross 1985). In part, this mystery is the result of U.S. government data collection practices that make it difficult to identify women involved in farming and ranching. By adhering to very narrow definitions of farm operator, which usually assume the male to be the sole operator, census data have not provided much direct information concerning the roles or contributions of women on family farms. The only women who are visible are those who, as unmarried women, provide sole ownership and management of their farms and ranches. Nevertheless, and despite problems of invisibility in current census practices, agricultural efforts of married farm and ranch women appear directly related to agricultural productivity in a way which can be inferred from census data.

Unpaid Family Labor

The greatest area of contribution for agriculturally employed farm women in the U.S. census remains that of "unpaid family labor." Although representation in the category of unpaid laborer has declined since 1970, it continues to constitute the largest class of agricultural endeavor for resident farm and ranch women. Census data suggest that the contributions of these "unpaid" women are quite important to the economic well-being of family farms.

The fact that the contributions of this part of the labor force are unpaid means that they are invisible in terms of conventional economic analysis, but it does not mean that such contributions are without economic value. To the contrary, classification of the woman as an "unpaid family worker" on family farms is associated with a markedly higher value for products sold than is true for any other category of employment.[12] This means that women's unpaid labor is related to a high level of agricultural productivity. Indeed, the average product value can be three times greater on husband-wife farms in which the employed wife is directly involved in agriculture. The evidence from census data is inferential, but even these data suggest that the agricultural contribu-

tions of farm women have direct importance for farm income as
well as for other sources of income used in support of the ranch
or farm.

Off-Farm Employment

Rising costs of everything from equipment to food have had dramatic impacts on the structure of agricultural enterprises.[13] Among
these impacts has been the necessity for increasing numbers of
farm families to supplement income by working off the farm. At
present, more than one-half of the income of farm families comes
from off-farm labor. Much of this labor is provided by resident
farm women.

By 1980 approximately 50 percent of rural farm women and
75 percent of rural farm men were defined as in the labor force.
Although the figure has remained constant for men during the
last decade, farm women have steadily increased their representation. Of resident farm women employed off-farm, approximately
one in four works in agriculture, compared to one in two for employed off-farm men. These figures represent a net decline in agricultural employment for both men and women during the last
decade. Despite the overall decline in agricultural employment
opportunities, there have been dramatic changes in the structure
of women's employment that are contradictory to the overall
decline.

Agricultural Self-Employment

In a time of general contraction in agricultural employment opportunities, American farm and ranch women have actually increased their contributions in some areas of agricultural employment, in particular self-employment. Since 1970 there have been
proportionate and absolute increases in agricultural self-
employment for farm women (Maret and Copp 1982). Propor-
tionately, agricultural self-employment for farm women doubled
in the past decade, while in absolute terms representation in agri-
·cultural self-employment increased by more than one-third. In contrast, male farm residents employed in agriculture experienced a
slight decline in self-employment. This leads to an expectation
that agriculturally related opportunities for women could be expanding. This expectation is contradictory to expectations derived
from the rural development literature that anticipate a decline in

the representation of women with increases in technological advancement. It would appear that there could be something happening to women's roles because of technological change. This expectation of changes in women's representation and roles is further suggested by census data regarding farm operators. While the farm population as a whole has been declining, the proportion of farm operators who are women has actually increased (Maret and Copp 1982). Over six percent of all farm operators are identified as women and 85 percent of male operators have wives present. Indeed, there is reason to suspect that the census data provide a severe under-representation of women's economic contributions.

Census data are generally insufficient for looking at women's roles in agriculture. Given the assumption that when men are present on agricultural operations they are the main operator, there is relatively little that can be known from census data, and this knowledge is very inferential. However, some recent government data do allow the visibility of women.

A national study of farm and ranch women undertaken as a joint venture between the USDA and NORC provides a direct look at the roles of farm and ranch women. These national survey data allow for an analysis of women's contributions to the labor and management of family owned agricultural operations, including ranches. Since this is a national sample of farm and ranch women, the present analysis of their contributions pertains to a broader base than the more narrow focus on ranching women in chapter 3. The national findings should be used to provide a general background for the portraits of ranching women to follow.

Many of the women in the national sample reported long histories of living or working in agricultural settings: 59 percent said they had grown up on a farm or ranch. Of the respondents, 12 percent referred to their operations as ranches, rather than farms, orchards, etc. At the time of the survey 96 percent of these women were married. About one-third were currently employed off the farm.

Contributions to Agricultural Tasks
Using a list of twelve common farm tasks, including bookkeeping, animal care, various types of field work, marketing products, and supervising labor, women were asked about their contribu-

tions to the physical workload on their farms. A listing of these tasks is provided in Table 1 along with the percentage of women who indicate various levels of involvement.

The proportion of women doing a task depends on the nature of the task (Jones and Rosenfeld 1981). Most frequently, women regularly take care of the vegetable garden and animals for family consumption (74 percent), do the bookkeeping (61 percent), and run farm errands (47 percent). These findings are consistent with those of small-scale surveys. It could well be that these tasks are of increasing importance to the modern family farm as we move further into the age of the computer and the "go-fer."[14]

Taking care of farm animals and helping with harvesting are tasks done at least occasionally by over half of the women whose farms include these tasks. Slightly less than half (42 percent) do other field work at least occasionally and supervise family members (49 percent). Between 30 and 40 percent report involvement in plowing and other field work with machines, making major purchases, supervising hired hands, and marketing products. Women are less likely to apply chemicals, but 17 percent do even this task at least occasionally.

On average, married women report being at least occasionally involved in about half of the listed farm tasks done on their operations (Jones and Rosenfeld 1981). Individuals vary considerably around this average. However, extreme cases are rare: 5 percent report involvement in all the tasks, while only 2 percent report contributing to none of the physical farm tasks on their operations. Nationwide, two-thirds of farm women report moderate levels of task involvement, doing from 20 to 80 percent of the tasks listed for their farms. A few, 13 percent, indicate relatively low levels of contribution, doing less than 20 percent of the tasks. A substantial 17 percent of married farm women perform more than 80 percent of the tasks done on their operations. These tasks are in addition to the household tasks, performed regularly by 97 percent of the farm women. All in all, significant proportions of the resident farm women participate in the physical work in their operations, including field work. There is, however, considerable variability among individual women, as well as by tasks.[15]

Contributions to Agricultural Decisions
In addition to the physical labor required on American farms and ranches, another crucial factor influencing the success of agricul-

tural enterprises is decision making. Decisions about what to produce, on what scale, and with what marketing strategy are essential to success. To take part in these decisions is certainly to make an important contribution to the enterprise. To what extent then do America's farm women contribute not only labor but also management expertise?

All respondents in the national survey were asked about decision patterns for nine specific areas, including six basic farm management decisions and three household management decisions. Table 2 lists the decision areas and presents the percentages of women who reported various degrees of involvement for each type of decision.

A very small minority of married women indicate sole authority for all the production decisions involving land purchase, sale, or rental; the purchase of major equipment; new production practices; when to market; or what to produce. However, substantial proportions of American farm and ranch women report sharing decision responsibilities in these areas. Women are least likely to participate in decisions about whether to buy major farm equipment, produce something new, sell products, or try a new production practice. However, even in these types of decisions, from 38 to 48 percent contribute. Indeed, 18 percent of the women surveyed reported making 100 percent of the decisions on their operations, either alone or jointly with spouses.

On average, married women are more likely to contribute to decisions than to make them alone. There appears to be somewhat less individual variation with regard to decision making contributions than with regard to task contributions. Farming decisions tend to be made by husbands *and* wives on America's family-owned farms and ranches. However, there is considerable variability among farm and ranch women, and some of this variability could be associated with the type of operation. One of the questions raised in chapter 3 is whether ranch women differ from farm women in their level of involvement.

Summary

Findings from census data suggest that women's contributions to agriculture are increasing, and that these contributions are essential to the productivity and the economic well-being of American farms. Not only do farm women increasingly support farming en-deavors with off-farm income, but their direct agricultural con-tributions appear to pay off in higher productivity yields.

Married women contribute to most of the tasks of their opera-tions at least on an occasional basis. Furthermore, women's con-tributions to farming may be increasing insofar as bookkeeping and "go-fering" are of growing importance to modern agricultural operations. America's farm women also participate in most of the farming decisions, including decisions about land, equipment, products, practices, and marketing.

Given these facts of productivity and involvement, one is tempted to conclude that the invisibility of American farm women must be lessening. However, observed facts of productivity and involvement are not sufficient for the recognition of women as agricultural producers. Surely, some important changes have been made in the tax codes and inheritance laws, but the changes are long overdue, too few, and often uninformed by the magnitude of women's efforts.

The operation of America's farms and ranches is most often a family function, shared to varying degrees by husbands and wives. American farm women occupy virtually every point on the farm involvement continuum, from noninvolvement, through equal sharing with a spouse, to single-handed management. Yet only those at the very highest involvement levels have been afforded recognition as operators and managers. There are many questions remaining about women's productive roles in agriculture.

The beef cattle industry is an industry of historic and contem-porary importance. It is important as a way of business, and it is important as a way of life. Beef cattle began to be important to the life and business of Texans before the Civil War, and beef cattle remain the number one agricultural product of the state of Texas. Ranching was a way of life for the early families of Texas, and it is also a way of life for families living on approximately 150,000 Texas ranches today. Much is known about the business of raising and selling cattle in Texas. Much less is known about the productive roles of women in ranching.

2

Ranching Women of the Past

A HISTORIC INDUSTRY, 1800–1950

The fact that women and men in agriculture do not have identical activity profiles or that, on average, married farm men have higher involvement levels in physical tasks than married farm women, is not alone sufficient to explain the exclusion of women from research and writing and even consciousness about their agricultural contributions. Peggy Ross (1984, 19) describes a "knowledge gap" about women's participation in agricultural production to be the result of a "tendency for researchers and policy makers to see farm-women primarily from the traditional viewpoint, as occupants of home and hearth roles." Furthermore, many sociological studies approach the study of farm women as wives and mothers rather than as agricultural producers. This is particularly true for studies prior to 1979.[1]

According to Sachs, farm women's positions have been influenced by an ideology of women's domesticity that devalues the participation of women in farm labor and management. Sachs notes that with few exceptions "the studies on decision making and the sexual division of labor on family farms assume that the primary contribution that women make on farms is noneconomic. Even when women's subsistence production is noted, it is underappreciated" (1983, 34). The traditional view of women focuses on their domestic responsibilities to the exclusion of their productive contributions. Ironically, the "traditional" view of women's roles is predominantly from an urban-industrial perspective, which presumes separate spheres of activity for women and men. The traditional view of women is that of domestic specialist and helpmate to men. Men are defined and perceived as the economic providers and producers.

The nominal designation of "cattleman" is but one element of linguistic usage in a culture that tends to ignore the productive roles of women. Linguistic customs reflect the notion that whatever else they do, women are, first and foremost, homemakers who consume rather than produce goods and services.[2] In industry or in agriculture men are still viewed as the primary breadwinners and producers. There is the rancher, and there is his wife – the ranch wife is not perceived to have the occupation of rancher.[3]

Historians and writers of popular historical fiction are part of this culture. The epic and historical accounts of the Texas beef cattle industry seldom refer to the economic contributions of women.[4] Is this because women were not there or were there only in limited roles? Or is this another "peculiar eclipsing" of women's productive roles?

Spanish Ranching Women

The tending of livestock from horseback dates back to the early 1700s in Texas. According to Myres, "The three colonial powers – Spain, France, and England – despite differences in frontier techniques and institutions, all utilized the ranch as a means for holding vast areas of unoccupied land with few men" (1969, 8). In Texas, early cattle ranching was dominated by the Spanish missions and the Catholic Franciscan priests (padres) who ran them. It was also a time of frequent Indian raids, first by the Apaches and then by the Comanches and their allies among the northern tribes, and of open hostilities between the civilian settlers and the Spanish military. Perhaps, for these reasons, one would expect few women in the Spanish ranching era, but this expectation would be wrong.

In 1731 sixteen families were sent to Texas from the Canary Islands by the Spanish crown. One of these settlers, María Bentacour, who became the founder of modern San Antonio, was among the first ranching women of Texas (Winegarten 1985). Another ranching woman of the eighteenth century, Doña Rosa Hinojosa de Balli, owned a vast ranch in the Rio Grande Valley with headquarters at La Feria and Ojo de Agua. She was granted 53,140.80 acres in her own name by Spain in 1777 (Taylor 1976, 6). Doña Rosa's son was the padre for whom Padre Island is named (Jackson 1986, 446–47). Ana María del Carmen Calvillo obtained three leagues and a labor of land across the river from present-day

Floresville (Jackson 1986, 413). She is reported to have ridden a white stallion and to have been shrewd and diplomatic in dealing with the Indians, who never attacked her ranch (Winegarten 1985, 12).

A more systematic demographic portrait of Spanish ranching women is provided by a ranch census of 1810 (in Jackson 1986, app. I). Of thirty independent resident ranches in this census, five were owned by women, twenty-two were owned by husbands and wives, and three were owned by men (two by widowers, one of whom lived with his mother-in-law). Among the women noted as the owners of ranches (with no husband present) were Doña Manuela Montes, Doña Josefa de la Garza, Barbara Sanchez, Doña Estacia Sambrano, and Doña María Feliciana Duran. Women were visible and important in the development of ranching from the early days of Spanish ranching.

Profiles of Women on the Texas Frontier

Lizzie Johnson, sometimes referred to as the "queen of cattle ranching" (Crawford and Ragsdale 1982, 132), began her career as a teacher and writer and was one of the women to take cattle herds up the Chisholm Trail from Texas to Saint Louis. Lizzie parlayed her real estate and cattle holdings into a fortune. When Lizzie married at age thirty-six, her husband signed a waiver to any rights to her property. Of her business acumen it was said by her male associates in the cattle business: "Oh, she was smart, knew cattle; knew when to buy and when to sell" (Crawford and Ragsdale 1982, 128). Between 1879 and 1889 Lizzie Johnson and Margaret Burland were two Texas ranch women who owned the herds they took up the Chisholm Trail.

Amanda Burks was a ranch woman from Banquete who went up the trail in the early 1870s (Crawford and Ragsdale 1982, 129). There are many other women who went up the cattle trails, usually with husbands. In *Interwoven* Sallie Reynolds Matthews writes about her sister Bettie (Lucinda Elizabeth Matthews Reynolds) and brother George, who traveled with trail herds to Colorado and California:[5]

> In this same year of 1868, my oldest brother, George, decided to go West and began to get together an outfit, wagons, oxen, men and horses. He had been working and trading since

he was a mere youth, and with some help from his father had accumulated seven or eight hundred cattle of his own. Added to these was his wife's dowry of two hundred nice young cattle that her father had given her, which made a fair sized herd.

There were many preparations to be made. An Army ambulance was bought and fitted up with a bed and other thaings for Sister Bettie's comfort. . . . These old-fashioned ambulances were heavy, cumbersome vehicles with three seats, used for transportation of officers and their families. . . . Sister Bettie drove the ambulance team most of the time on the trip. (1936, 57)

According to Worcester (1987), Mrs. Jackson Squires came from Illinois to buy Texas cattle in 1854. She, her husband, her father, and her brother bought six hundred Longhorn steers near Houston. They crossed the Mississippi at Hannibal, Missouri, reaching their farm near present-day Riverside, Illinois, after several months on the trail.

Mary Taylor Bunton was a well-educated woman who ranched with her husband near Sweetwater, Texas. Mary joined her husband on a trail drive in 1886 and described her experiences in *A Bride on the Old Chisholm Trail*, first published in 1939. Some of these recollections depict the serenity and slow pace of the long trail drive, whose object was to get fat cattle to market: "The first part of the trip was perfect in weather and in interest. It was a novel sight to see those immense herds of cattle slowly winding their way along the trail. Riding ahead of the herd I would turn in my saddle and look back, and it would look as if the entire face of the earth was just a moving mass of heads and horns" (p. 240). There were, however, less serene aspects of the trail drive, as Bunton notes:

All Spring the weather had been very warm and rattlesnakes were to be seen and heard everywhere. . . . I had to watch out every moment, for even as I rode along they would hiss as they lay alongside the road, coiled ready to strike. Giant rattlers, sometimes as many as six or eight by actual count would be coiled beneath the shade of the trees enjoying the sunlight and growing warm. . . . One day, Mr. Bunton decided to count the cattle in the herd behind us, so I went with him. We were returning to camp, and, as usual after a day's trip we were tired and hungry, so we sat down near the chuck wagon and old Sam was serving us supper when one of the cowboys came up and kindly offered to spread our blankets for the night. It was a little to dark for him to see the ground plainly, so he spread the tarpaulin and blankets over a rattlesnakes hole without knowing it. In the night, the snake, I suppose, got too warm or possibly hungry, so it crawled out of its hole, and as it could not get out from under the tarpaulin because of the weight of our bodies, it stretched its body full length between us. As usual, the next morning we were up before day, and as it began to get near daylight, I chanced to notice the ridge under our blankets. I spoke of it to Mr. Bunton only to be laughed at for my fears. He assured me the ridge was nothing more than a small branch of tree that George failed to see when he spread our blankets the night before. His explanation failed to satisfy me, so I lingered around to see for myself, and sure enough, when the blankets were rolled away for the day, there we found his snakeship peacefully sleeping. We were so amazed and yet so thankful that he had not bitten us that we allowed the five foot diamond back rattler with its many rattles and a button to crawl back into its hole unharmed! (p. 250)

In 1854 another well-educated woman, Henrietta Chamberlain, married Richard King and went to live in a new cow camp described as "an irregularly shaped piece of wilderness measuring three and one half square Spanish leagues" (Lea, 1957, 103) located about forty-five miles southwest of present-day Corpus Christi. Henrietta was twenty-two years old. Decades later she wrote of her first days at the ranch:

> When I came as a bride in 1854, the little ranch home then— a mere "jacal" as the Mexicans would call it—was our abode for many months until our main ranch dwelling was completed. But I doubt if it falls to the lot of many a bride to have had so happy a honeymoon. On horseback we roamed the broad prairies. When I grew tired my husband would spread a Mexican blanket for me and then I would take my siesta under the shade of the mesquite tree. . . . At first our cattle were long horns from Mexico. We had no fences and branding was hard work. (Lea 1957, 128)

From the day of her arrival at Santa Gertrudis, Henrietta King seemed to have been at home (see Lea 1957, 129). The ranch workers, or "Kineños," called her La Madame or La Patrona. Despite the primitive and sometimes dangerous conditions, "no roughness discouraged the captain's wife from residence at the ranch"

(Lea 1957, 147). Indeed, Henrietta often "rode a spring wagon to the gathering of herds" (Lea 1957, 150). The first of the King Ranch brands officially recorded in the brand registry of Nueces County on March 20, 1859, consisted of the connected initials of Henrietta King (HK).

At this time, ranch operation remained primitive: "Ranching was simply the ownership of branded herds roughly controlled on unfenced prairie near a possessed supply of scarce and precious water. . . . The only cattle a rancher owned were cattle half-wild, quick and fierce, armed with long horns and hard to handle." (Lea 1957, 148)

Together Henrietta and Richard King built one of the most prominent ranches in the state of Texas and the country. It is likely that the "largely unread" (Lea 1957, 139) Richard King relied heavily upon the abilities of an educated Henrietta. Certainly, Richard relied on Henrietta to run the ranch during the times of his prolonged absence, including the Civil War. After the Civil War, "the raiding of Texas ranches and the theft of almost incredible number of Texas livestock was continuous from 1865 until 1878" (Lea 1957, 264). Henrietta was frequently in charge during this era because Richard King's business meant he "had to travel constantly" (Lea 1957, 271). It is said of the Patrona, Henrietta King, that ". . . so resolute a woman was she that it was said the outlaws and renegades who infested the neighborhood preferred to approach the house when Captain King was at home rather than to try it when his wife was there alone" (Lea 1957, 131).

When Richard King died in 1885, the ranch encompassed 600,000 acres and was heavily in debt. It is legend that "King left his widow half a million acres along with half a million dollars debt" (Lea 1957, 471). In her forty years of sole ownership, Henrietta Chamberlain King built the ranch to more than 1,175,000 acres and 94,000 head of cattle (Nixon 1986, 22). She continued to practice the advice of a dear family friend, Robert E. Lee, to buy land and never to sell it.

The King Ranch was and is among the most prominent ranches in Texas. The townsite of Kingsville was donated by Henrietta King and is named after the ranch. The King Ranch also is distinguished by its own breed of cattle, named after the creek, the Santa Gertrudis. In 1940 the USDA recognized the Santa Gertrudis breed of cattle as "the first beef breed ever produced in America. . . ." (Nixon 1986, 27).

Molly Goodnight, another pioneer ranch woman, helped establish the first ranch in the Texas Panhandle in 1877. The Goodnights called their ranch the J A ranch. Their closest neighbor was seventy-five miles distant. It was Molly whose loneliness was so great that when she received a gift of three live chickens to cook for dinner, "she kept them as pets instead" (Winegarten 1985, 56). Molly maintained a separate herd of cattle with her own brand, registered in Texas and in Colorado. She was among the first cattle ranchers to be interested in purebred cattle. Molly also raised the buffalo calves left orphaned by the hunters, and she may have been the first to cross cattle with buffalo. With the death of the Goodnight's financial partner in 1885, the Goodnights moved to establish a third ranch in northeast Armstrong County. In 1898 Molly's interest in education led to the establishment of Goodnight College, located across the hill from their ranch. In twentieth-century Texas, the Goodnight ranch with its herds of buffalo, crossbred "cattalo," and fine Shorthorn cattle became a tourist attraction (Crawford and Ragsdale 1982, 119).

Hallie Crawford Stillwell: A Living Legend

Hallie Crawford Stillwell no longer has the strength of body needed to run a West Texas cattle ranch and has turned much of the management over to her heirs. Fortunately, the power of her words is in no way diminished by her eighty-six years of experiences as a rancher, justice of the peace, and chronicler of the Big Bend. At the age of twelve Hallie drove a covered wagon with a team of four horses to Alpine where her family settled into the mercantile business and where Hallie attended public school. At twenty she married Roy Stillwell and moved to his ranch along the rugged border territory. Here her ranching career began as she rode with the cowboys to help contain the cattle on the two hundred sections of land and to escape the bandits who still raided across the border. Hallie has so many "ranch tales and cowboy stories" that it is difficult to select among them. Here are two that reflect the strength and courage of pioneer Texas ranch women as well as the challenges which confronted them when their menfolk were not around.[6]

Some of Hallie's stories confirm the presence of bandits late into the twentieth century. Hallie's sister-in-law, Alice Stillwell

Henderson, had many encounters with unfriendly Mexican soldiers and with bandits from 1878, when the Stillwells drove the
first cattle herd into northern Mexico, until 1895 when they crossed
their last head of stock to the Texas side. During that period Mrs.
Henderson crossed the border alone to recapture her husband's
stolen Winchester and saddle from Mexican soldiers. After con-
fronting the men at gunpoint and recovering the rifle and saddle,
Mrs. Henderson made a successful escape by hiding herself and
her horse in a herd of cattle: "In a few minutes, the captain and
his soldiers thundered by on their horses, following the trail toward
the river, while Alice Stillwell Henderson watched from her hiding place among the milling herd. After her pursuers were out
of sight, she mounted and took another trail to the Rio Grande,
which she crossed several hours later undetected" (Madison 1955,
116–18).

Hallie also describes the tasks performed by women on the remote cattle ranches of West Texas fifty years later, when women
picked up the roles vacated by men. Virginia Madison writes:

> When World War II came on, and the cowboys and sons of
> the cattlemen began to hang up their chaps and spurs and put
> saddle soap on their saddles to protect them until they "came
> home," the ranchwomen filled the vacancies. There was the
> greatest demand for beef the world had ever known, and there
> was less labor and concentrated cattle feed with which to raise
> cattle to supply the demand. A great deal was heard about the
> wonderful work being done on farms and in factories by women
> during the wartime, but little was said about the women on
> the range. (1955, 130)

Hallie then tells in her own words about life on a cattle ranch
in the Big Bend area during the 1940s:

> Living on a cattle ranch in the Big Bend country isn't all riding
> horseback in the moonlight over bridle paths. When my eldest
> son went to war in 1941, I took up the stirrups of his saddle,
> appropriated his mounts, and decided I would do my best to
> take his place on our ranch, caring for about a thousand head
> of cattle ranging over an area of two hundred sections of land,
> situated in one of the roughest and wildest parts of the Big
> Bend. We were a team of three, my husband, our younger son,
> Guy, and myself. Teamwork, of course, was our only hope to
> keep the ranch going during the war years. We mastered all
> the short cuts of management and held our little layout to-

gether in spite of rationing and OPA and shortages of materials and labor. Riding the range here is no child's play, for it
extends over miles and miles of rough, rocky, brushy, cactusy,
mountainous country. To find the scattered cattle requires skill,
hard work, patience, fortitude, and hard riding. After they are
gathered, the work in the corral requires the skill of seasoned
cowpunchers.

When the war came on, I was no green hand on the ranch
for I had worked, along with my husband and sons, for twenty-
five years, gradually letting the hardest work fall to the boys,
but when one son was claimed by the armed forces the hard
labor of cattle raising again was thrust upon me.

We live forty-six miles from Marathon, where we got our
mail and ranch supplies. It is seventy-six miles to Alpine, the
county seat, where we do our banking and business, which
means that we had to travel seventy-six miles to visit the ration
board and the OPA. Forty-six miles of this was over rough,
rocky, dirt road. With tire rationing and gas rationing, it was
not a pleasant business. In addition to my cowpunching duties,
I did all my own cooking on a wood stove, tended a small garden, milked a cow, and raised a few chickens. In my spare time,
I did our laundry and the housework. (Madison 1955, 130)

Hallie recounts that the arduous tasks of roundup required skill,
courage, and resoluteness of purpose as well as strength of body.
Although she was no greenhand, working cattle is dangerous business. Despite the hardships and the extra burdens brought on
by war, Hallie maintained a sense of humor as she went about
the ranch work. In working cows, luck is often the difference between serious harm and "a good story":

Our hardest ranchwork comes in the fall, when we round
up to brand the calves, and that is when the highlights and
ranch work take place. The three of us would saddle up about
sunrise and ride out into the pasture and get together what
cattle we could handle in the pen for one day's work. It was
usually about one or two o'clock in the afternoon before we
could get a herd to the pens. We then would snatch a bite to
eat and immediately get to work with the branding.

Roy, on his favorite roping horse, Red, heeled the calves with
his rope. Guy and I would throw and tie them down. We usually tied down about six calves before we started working on
them. One of us would grab him by the tail, while the other
one grabbed the rope, and with split-second timing we both

would give a stiff yank and the calf went down. The one who did the tailing held the calf by the top foreleg and sat on the calf's top side while the other took a small tie rope and tied three of the calf's feet together. This sounds simple, but, if you think there is no skill attached to such a performance, try it sometime. One has to be in the right place at the right time and do the right thing or there may be disastrous results.

One day I made a bobble and had one hand about two inches too far over the calf's back and it kicked me on the hand. Guy and I both heard the bone when it broke but I held on to the calf. Before Guy could get him tied my hand was swollen twice its natural size. It hurt pretty bad but I didn't say anything for I knew I had to keep on with the work. There was no one to take my place. The next calf that Roy heeled was a big heifer and I knew she would be bad so I let Guy tail her over and I grabbed the rope with such force it slipped off her two hind feet and I lost my balance, turning a backward flip right under Red's belly. Thank goodness, Red is a good, gentle, and smart horse or he would have kicked me to pieces. I was pretty mad by that time and almost in tears. With a broken hand and bruised all over from a hard fall, I started for the gate to call it quits when I thought of son over in England risking his life every day. The next calf Roy roped I was on the job to tail him over and hold down while Guy tied him.

After we got a string of calves tied down we started the works on them. Guy did the branding, with a hot iron, Roy did the ear marking and castrating, while I did the vaccinating for blackleg. Then we all three did the dehorning, which is the most tedious job of all. We clipped the horns off with a clipper device, seared the wound over with a hot iron until the bleeding stopped, and dabbed on some medicine. Then all the calves had to be untied and "turned up" as we call it. Some of them got up fighting mad, especially the bulls which had just been made into steers. Sometimes they charged us and we had to climb the fence. Then we tied down another string of six and the same routine was followed.

Late one fall, during the war, we had some two-year-old bulls to brand. They were salty and I knew we were going to hub hell with them. The first one Roy heeled was plenty mad. Guy tailed him over and I grabbed a tie rope to tie him down. I put the rope on his front foot but before I could jerk back he landed me on the jaw with his hind foot. I saw stars, slacked the rope enough to let him start kicking, and, before I could get the rope wrapped, it began to slip through my hand. There was no knot on the end, so it slipped right on through, giving me painful rope burn in the palm of my hand. I am not prone to using vile language, but that time I cussed for all I could think of and almost shocked my husband out of the saddle.

That night I had to sleep on a bedroll in the bed of a truck, because we were camped out on that job ten miles from our headquarters. Before daybreak, the cold wind started blowing, and numbness from cold was added to my other miseries of an aching and swollen jaw, a stiff, rope-burned hand, and bodily bruises too numerous to mention. I got out of my bedroll and built a campfire and put the coffee on. Three cups of black coffee thawed me out and my jaw got limber enough to allow me to talk; so I was able to continue with the works, talking, tailing, and riding. (Madison 1955, 131–33)

Systematic Evidence about Women's Presence on the Frontier

There are early censuses which suggest the presence of women.[7] There are records from the Texas Department of Agriculture Family Land Heritage Program that document women among the pioneer settlers of ranches, including single women. Some of these women established ranching families which are still influential in the modern cattle industry. There are also the testimonies of women recorded in pioneer chronicles and the experiences recalled by the older women interviewed in this research. These women lived the rugged, rustler-fighting days of the early Texas cattle industry.[8]

Evidence from Historical Census Data

Demographic evidence presented below indicates that as early as 1850 women comprised 46.5 percent of the population of Texas. Moreover, the distribution of women was fairly uniform among counties, including those considered to be "frontier counties." Table 3 reports the sex-composition for all Texas counties of two hundred or more inhabitants from 1850 to 1880. Men did outnumber women in most counties, but not to the exaggerated extent suggested in popular fiction, which is, indeed, often accepted as historical fact. In only a few counties was the representation of women less than one-third of the total population. In *no* case

does the representation of women appear so low as to warrant
the myth of a masculine state or even a masculine frontier. Even
in those counties of the "wild" West Texas frontier (indicated by
a single asterisk on Table 3), women were present. By 1880 the
populace of El Paso County was approximately one-half female.
In 1880 Pecos County was 41 percent female and Presidio County
was approaching 40 percent. Texas women may be invisible to
the popular writers of Texas history and even to more serious historians, but women were visible to the census takers. This is systematic evidence of the presence of women in the early days of
statehood. There are other data to augment the demographics.

Evidence from the Texas Family Land Heritage Program
Data from the Land Heritage Program of the Texas Department
of Agriculture provide information on ranches which have been
in continuous agricultural production and maintained by the same
family for a century or more. Many of these ranches were founded
by women and have been maintained by women through succes-
sive generations of agricultural production. These data are consistent with observations that "a quarter of a million women ran
farms of their own" (Sachs 1983, 16) in the last quarter of the nine-
teenth century. Among the founding ranchers in Texas were Mrs.
August Schoenewolf, Lucinda A. Shelton, Adeline Hinton, Rachel
Ann Northington Hudgins, and Mrs. Ann Burke.

In 1855, at the time the 320-acre Luckenbach Ranch, in Gillespie County, was settled by Mrs. August Schoenewolf, Sr., of
Kaltengsfeld, Germany, Central Texas was rugged territory. Herds
ran on the open range, and the danger of Indian raids was constant. Not much is reported about the life of the founder, but
Mrs. Benno Luckenbach, great-great-niece of Mrs. Schoenewolf,
is said to have farmed from horse and mule, switching to tractors
and modern farming equipment when they became available. The
ranch is presently owned and operated by Miss Clara Anna Louise
Luckenbach, who raises feed and grain to feed the Hereford cattle,
sheep, and poultry on her land.

There is a long-standing and well-imbedded notion that women
manage agricultural operations because of the death of spouses.
Certainly, women on average do outlive men, but this is not to
say that women are ranchers only because of the death of their
spouses. Women also inherit land from their parents and pass it
on to their female as well as their male children. In 1843 the Lati-

mer Ranch was established with part of the eight hundred acres given to Lucinda A. Shelton by her father. Today the ranch is owned and operated by three sisters (Theresa May, Elizabeth, and Lucy) who raise hay and livestock on the land inherited from their mother.

The hardiness of pioneer women is reflected in the life of the co-founder of the Hinton Ranch in Gonzales County. Adeline Hinton of Alabama was married in 1848 and gave birth to ten children from 1849 to 1874. In 1872 she and her husband, Robertus R. Hinton, settled 348 acres and produced grain and cotton in addition to cattle. During this time the first herd drives began in Gonzales, and Mr. Hinton was often gone; so there were extended periods of time in this sparsely populated area when Mrs. Hinton ranched alone. Now a granddaughter, Miss Lillian L. Hinton, of Gonzales, manages the ranch (TDA Family Land Heritage Program 1974).

Of the heritage properties listed in the Texas Land Heritage Program, approximately fifty were founded by single women. The majority were founded by women and their husbands. Approximately one-third were founded by single men. Although the norm for the early foundation settlements was for married women and men, single women were by no means absent from the hardships and challenges of establishing Texas farms and ranches. Some of these women later established ranching families that expanded and branched in succeeding generations into major and multiple heritage holdings.

Such a woman was Rachel Ann Northington Hudgins, who purchased 10,827 acres in Wharton County in 1882, nine years after the death of her husband, Joel Hudgins. Her purchase gave rise to five ranching families around Hungerford, Texas, including two of the major ranching families in Texas today: the divisions of the H. D. Hudgins Ranch credited with the origination and establishment of the American Brahman breed of cattle, and the Real McCoy Farm, which through several generations has been a leader in the commercial cattle industry. Rachel Ann came to Texas from Kentucky in 1831. With her father, she lived on a 4,428-acre league, acquired as a land grant from the government of Mexico, in what is now Fort Bend County. In 1847 Rachel Ann married Joel Hudgins. In 1852 she recorded her own cattle brand as a half-circle running M. Today her great grandson uses this same brand. Rachel Ann bore nine children. Four sons survived to adulthood and recorded their brands in 1874. One son, Josiah Dawson (J. D.), bought several head of Brahman cattle from the original importation by the Shanghai Pierce Estate (See the interview of Mrs. Ethel Williams, in the next chapter, who ranches today in the country of Shanghai Pierce). J. D.'s heirs continued to raise Brahman cattle on the Hudgins Ranch and at one time owned more registered American gray Brahman than any other ranch in the world. The Real McCoy Farm is also owned by descendants of Rachel Ann, as are the Forgason Ranch, the Koonce-Cullers Ranch, and the Mangum Ranch.

The Little Burke Ranch in Bee County, Texas, was founded in 1835 by Mrs. Ann Burke of Tipperary, Ireland. Despite the death of her husband during the journey to America and the birth of a child "only one hour after the ship reached American shores on the Texas coast," Ann persevered to stake a claim and to raise cattle and horses on "a widow's grant of one labor and one league" (TDA Family Land Heritage Program 1981, 3), 150 acres of which Ann Burke later gave to the townsite of Beeville (a labor and a league equal approximately 4,600 acres). In 1861 Ann deeded one-half league of her land to her son Patrick for $100. Patrick and his wife, Nancy, had four sons and four daughters. One of the daughters, Clara, took over approximately 2,500 acres in 1912. Clara married John Wilson and they had five children, three boys and two girls. In 1943 the current owner, Clara Elizabeth (Ray), received 490 acres of family land (TDA Family Land Heritage Program 1981, 3). Today, the land supports commercial crossbred Hereford-Brahman cattle and is operated by Mrs. Ray and her sons, Robert and Wilson.

Women were sometimes the founders and often the retainers of the ranching heritage of Texas. Research of the Family Land Heritage Program is summarized in Table 4. These data provide a more systematic overview of the representation of women in the program.

Overall, women own and often operate 24 percent of the heritage farms and ranches. In partnership with men, usually brothers or husbands, the representation of women increases to 66 percent or two-thirds of the Texas heritage properties.

In the modern era, as on the frontier, the norm is women and men working together–ranching together. Certainly, the number of single men who own heritage properties is higher than that of single women. However, it is interesting to note that, in spite of the stereotype of the male farmer and rancher, in three years of the Family Land Heritage Program (1975, 1981, and 1983) a slightly higher percentage of properties inducted into the program were owned and operated by single women than by single men. Although the Family Land Heritage Program is not representative of all Texas farms and ranches, it does provide reliable and systematic evidence of women's presence as the owners of Texas cattle ranches, from pioneer times to the present.

3

A Continuing Legacy

RANCHING WOMEN, 1950-80

The successful commercial cattleman in America today has to be smarter than ever before. Every day he is faced with a wealth of new information that could affect the efficiency of his daily operations. He tries to understand the economy. He fights the environment and weather. He struggles with political debates. And he attempts to solidify the value of his product. Nothing is taken for granted and he has to stand tall and make firm hard-line decisions. Decisions that cannot be wrong. These are the people that make up the backbone of America's commercial cattle industry. These are the tough customers.

—BRANGUS 1990

The Status and Roles of Resident Ranch Women

Women occupy an important status as ranch owners. Women were present as landowners on the frontier, and women have helped to preserve ranches owned by the same families through generations of continuous production. At present, women own or co-own about two-thirds of all ranch property. Moreover, women on contemporary ranches perform the same kinds of physical tasks and engage in the same kinds of managerial decisions as ranching men. Women own cattle ranches, work the cattle, and make production and marketing decisions.

Women as Land Owners

Evidence from the Family Land Heritage Program in chapter 2 indicates women are the sole owners of approximately one in four Texas ranches. In some cases women own ranches with other women, with sisters and daughters, but ownership is not shared with men in 24 percent of the Heritage properties. Approximately 43 percent of Texas ranches are co-owned by women and men. Sometimes these men are husbands; sometimes they are brothers or sons. While women and men do own and operate ranches separately, the norm appears to be women and men ranching together.

Additional evidence regarding women's status as land owners is available from the USDA-NORC national survey of farm and ranch women. From these data it is possible to identify fifty-five women ranchers living on ranches in the Southwestern United States. All of these women are married. In other words, these women are part of ranching families. Of these women, 88 percent report that their name is on the land deed or ranch title.[1] They are ranch owners.

Though valuable, the information on land ownership says nothing about women's roles as ranchers. It could be argued that while women own the ranches, it is still men who manage them and men who do the labor—the men who are "the tough customers." What can be said about the work done by women on jointly owned ranches?

Women as Ranch Operators and Laborers
Of the fifty-five Southwestern women ranchers identified in the USDA-NORC survey, 52 percent report that they definitely would be able to run the operation on their own. Another 32 percent say they would probably be able to run the operation on their own. This finding suggests that women on ranches consider themselves quite capable as ranch operators or hands.

Given a certain ambiguity about the meaning of main operator, even more direct evidence about women's contributions to ranch work is provided by the data in Table 5. This table reports the extent to which women participate in various ranch tasks.[2] Although many routine jobs such as fence mending and heat detection (telling when cows are ready to be bred) are not included in this survey, there is an interesting portrait of contributions to routine farm tasks. It would appear that married ranch women are most likely to contribute to activities regularly performed on ranches, such as taking care of animals, running farm errands ("gofering"), purchasing major supplies, and marketing products. Their regular participation ranges from a high of 71 percent for keeping records to a low of 23 percent for purchasing major supplies. Ranching women also tend to contribute to subsistence activities, that is, growing vegetables or animals for home consumption on a regular basis (although not as frequently as do women on farms). Record keeping is of increasing importance on American cattle ranches, as is "go-fering," which is defined as the fine art of finding everything needed. Both of these are the regular domain of women. They also tend to contribute on a regular basis to marketing activities and to purchasing major supplies.

Compared with the farm women described in chapter 1, these Southwestern ranch women are less likely to plow, harvest crops, or tend to a garden or animals for family consumption (refer to Tables 1–4). They are somewhat more likely than farm women to supervise hired hands, purchase major supplies, market products, and keep records. They are about as likely as resident farm women to take care of animals, supervise family members, work on the family's in-home business, and run errands.

Women as Ranch Managers

In addition to ranch ownership and operation, another area of contribution is management or decision making. Women can contribute to ranch decisions. Do they? The data in Table 6 suggest that for married couples, ranching is a joint venture. Similar to the findings of studies for farm women (Sachs 1983, 31), these figures indicate that joint decision making is most prevalent in "resource decisions," particularly decisions involving land. Two-thirds of the respondents report that the decision to buy or sell land is a joint decision by the respondent and husband. Of those renting land, 71 percent say the decision to rent is made jointly. It is more likely that husbands alone make decisions about selling products, new production practices, purchasing major farm equipment, and trying new crops or livestock breeds. However, among the ranch families represented even these decisions are about as likely to be made jointly as to be made solely by husbands. The only decision which appears to be significantly more likely to be made by husbands is that of trying a new crop or breed of livestock. In this case, 54 percent of respondents report that this is usually the husband's decision compared with 44 percent who report that this is usually a joint decision. On the other hand, taking an off-farm job appears to be the respondent's domain: 44 percent of respondents report that deciding to take an off-farm job is her decision, while 46 percent say that the decision is made jointly. Less than 10 percent of respondents say that the decision for a wife to take an off-farm job is made by the husband.

Compared with all women in the USDA-NORC survey, ranch women are significantly more likely to enter into decisions about when to sell products (49 percent compared with 36 percent of all women), about trying new production practices (49 percent compared with 35 percent of all women), about buying and sell-ing land (66 percent compared with 58 percent for all women), and about renting land (71 percent compared with 50 percent for all women). The majority of ranching women enter into decisions regarding land, and with regard to these land decisions they are more involved in management than are women in other types of agricultural operations. Economic decisions related to off-farm employment and to land purchase, sale, and rental are particu-larly likely to involve ranching women. However, even decisions regarding production and equipment are likely to be made jointly by ranch women and their husbands. Ranching women are an integral part of contemporary ranching operations.

Despite the masculine image of ranching, women would ap-pear to be more involved in the ownership and management of ranching operations than is true, generally, for women farmers. However, ranching women are not significantly more likely than farm women to identify this involvement as their occupation. Only 13.3 percent of resident ranch women in the Southwest list their occupation as rancher on income tax forms. Approximately half (49.4 percent) list their occupation as wife-mother-homemaker. Another 37.3 percent list other occupations on tax forms. Thus, a majority of married ranch women would appear to agree with normative expectations regarding women's roles. They can co-own the land, do the work of ranchers, and participate in ranch man-agement, but many still identify with traditional female roles.

Influences on Women Choosing Ranching Occupations

In a sense, the seven Southwestern women who identify their oc-cupation as ranchers in the USDA-NORC survey have denied the sex-role stereotype of the cattleman, or at least defied it in their own lives. The remaining questions of this chapter focus on women who define themselves occupationally as ranchers.

Given that some women do self-identify ranching as their occupation, can certain characteristics or circumstances be identified among the women who have chosen what is considered a
"nontraditional" occupation for women? Do ranching women share
any circumstances or characteristics that could distinguish them
from women who choose more "traditional" female occupations,
such as nursing, teaching, or clerical work? The profiles of contemporary ranching women presented next expand on the rich
diversity of the women's experiences. One of the goals of this
research is to describe variability and difference. There are important differences in the characteristics and circumstances of
ranching women. However, for the moment, the search is for commonalities in their experiences.

Most of the ranching women I interviewed had the opportunity to be ranchers. The women inherited their ranches usually
from parents or, occasionally, from spouses. They shared the circumstance of opportunity. Ranching women also tend to share
characteristics associated with higher than average levels of labor
force participation (Maret 1983). They have, on average, more formal education than the general population of women. They are
also characterized by fairly small families of orientation—coming
from backgrounds with none or few, and usually female—siblings.
The women I interviewed were mostly brought up on a ranch doing ranch chores and sharing the responsibilities of ranch life.
There were both the expectation *and* the opportunity to be part
of the ranching way of life. For many, a sense of responsibility
and family continuity contributed to the ultimate decision to take
over and run the ranch. Many of these women expressed the feeling that ranches survive only because of their contributions. They
are the survivors—the "Keepers of the Land." Most feel that the
ranch will not survive beyond them.

In all cases where the women own and manage their ranches,
there was opportunity. Social scientists sometimes forget the importance of opportunity in the search for reasons and "choices"
in the selection of occupations. To have choice, there must be
opportunity. In most cases the women were born to a ranching
heritage. In one case, a purebred breeder, the woman bought into
ranching. However, because of the great cost involved in the initial purchase of both land and cattle, this has been a rare form
of entry for women and not that frequent for men. Again, there
is tremendous change in the industry, and ranching is, with in-

creasing frequency, combined with other occupations that pay for the cost of ranching.

In the past, the most usual form of entry into ranching was through direct inheritance of the ranch. All of the women profiled below own commercial cattle ranches inherited from their parents. The inheritance of ranching includes social as well as economic components. For many, ranching is a lifestyle—as much a matter of how to live as one of how to make a living. A love of ranching as a way of life leads the children of ranchers who are successful in occupations such as law, medicine, and even teaching back into the cattle business on a part-time basis.[3]

The literature on "nontraditional" occupational choice suggests some other circumstances shared by the ranching women. The "nontraditional" choices of a ranching career do emerge from "more advantaged backgrounds" (almost by definition). Poor people do not have large cattle ranches. The opportunity for inheritance may also explain the absence of minority cattlewomen.[4] The cattlewomen I interviewed do seem to have received "exceptional encouragement" from significant others—usually their parents.[5] In the sense that ranching women came from advantaged backgrounds in which their participation in ranching activities was encouraged, the present findings lend support to the "enrichment hypothesis" for women choosing nontraditional careers. Women entering the nontraditional occupation of beef cattle ranching do come from "enriched" backgrounds. This is true in the sense of family socioeconomic standing, the encouragement of significant others, and a higher than average degree of academic achievement. In many cases the father is also a model of occupational identification for ranching daughters.

As already noted, one of the major influences on women's occupations is the structure of opportunities. One simply cannot assume a model of "free choice" when these choices are circumscribed by conditions beyond the individual's control. For example, a woman applying to an all-male university will not be admitted regardless of her grade point, standing in high school, or her "choice" of a school. This was the circumstance for women applying to the Texas College of Veterinary Medicine until the 1960s. Hence, the nature of the industry in which women seek jobs is extremely important.

Bear in mind that the study reported below is not based on a random sample of ranching women. To the contrary, the sub-

jects were purposely selected because they satisfied certain criteria. They must clearly own the ranch (that is, the ranch must
be their "separate property"). They must clearly manage the ranch.
Many women were excluded here, particularly those who owned
the larger ranches, because they used hired labor, which confused
the question of who did what. Of course, if a male owner used
hired labor, we would still assume that the decisions were his.
They also must clearly perform all or most of the tasks on their
operations. This selection criterion favored women who owned
small and medium-sized ranches. It also favored women who were
ranch residents rather than those who commuted from a city or
town. Finally, a decision was made to focus on commercial cow-
calf operations. The commercial cow-calf operator is the backbone of the production segment of the industry. However, the
stocker-feeder operation and that of the purebred or seedstock
producer, which can be and often are combined with the commercial cow-calf operation, are also important to the production
segment of the industry.

Because the selection criteria were so stringent, it would seem
that very few women would remain from the selection process.
However, that was not the case. If time and money were available, I would still be interviewing ranching women who satisfy
all of the selection criteria listed above. The women profiled below
were chosen, in part, because they seemed representative of more
of the ranching women of the Texas range.

Profiles of Contemporary Ranching Women

Five women are profiled in the following pages. They are chosen
to represent the contemporary ranching women of Texas. They
are all ranchers who own and manage commercial cow-calf operations. All have inherited their ranches from parents—they are third-
or fourth-generation ranchers. All of them participate fully in the
tasks and decisions of their operations. Only two are currently
married. In terms of ranch size, theirs are neither the largest nor
the smallest. They represent the overwhelming majority of contemporary cattle producers who own in the range of fifty to two
hundred mother cows. They all would be recognized by the Bureau of the Census as "sole operators."

In a way, the required designation of "sole operator" is grossly unfair to the thousands of women who ranch with men—with fathers, brothers, husbands, and sons—and who share ranching tasks and decisions. The majority of ranchers today, as in frontier days, are members of families. The problem with looking at family ranches is that the husband (or other adult male) is presumed to be the rancher, while the woman is relegated to the secondary and supportive role of "rancher's wife." This is often the case in spite of the fact that the ranch may be the woman's by both inheritance and interest. Men are assumed to be the cattle producers, and, with few exceptions, men are visible in the cattle organizations and in the financial institutions. It is assumed that women "married to ranchers" are only supporting their ranching husbands.

One of my objectives was to give some visibility to the contributions made by ranching women. However, in order to accomplish this I found myself succumbing to the temptation to use the most obvious cases, that is, cases in which no men were present on the ranch. I did this in order to emphasize that the contributions were those of the woman. When women ranch alone, there is certainly greater agreement that they actually are the ranchers. However, most women do not ranch alone, nor do they live alone during the longest portion of their lives. They live and work with men. Herein lies the greater challenge: to suggest that women can be and are ranchers—sometimes the principal rancher—even when men are present in the household. This is true for both Angela Bonifazi and Martha Ann Clements Lawhorn, the two women who are presently married. Angela has always been the rancher in the family, running the ranch she inherited, while her husband worked off the ranch. Martha Ann also runs her own ranch, while her rancher-husband maintains his ranch a hundred miles away. They share equipment and provide help for each other, but each manages his or her own ranch.

These women do not fit the national "norm" in terms of their marital status. Only 40 percent of the ranching women profiled here are married, in contrast to the national statistical profile of farm and ranch women. Of the unmarried women in this chapter, one is widowed, one is divorced, and one has never married.[6]

There are commonalities among these women. They share certain personal characteristics: strength and self-sufficiency, a reluctance to give in or give up, and a certain "subjective aware-ness" of their own differences. They also share some background characteristics: few and only female siblings, strong father and mother figures, and parental support of their ranching interests. They all have been born to ranching as a way of life. Most have a strong sense of responsibility both to their families and to their ranching heritage. They share a strong liking for their cows and for the other "critters" of the Texas range.

They come from relatively small and intact families (from 0 to 2 siblings). The families of orientation, the families they grew up in, are traditional, with no instance of divorce. In keeping with the literature on women in nontraditional occupations, there is a strong father figure. Just as consistently, there is also a strong mother figure—although I usually had to probe for the mother's influence and contributions. The father, rather than the mother, is usually identified as the daughter's "role model."

These ranching women tend to share a relatively conservative view of women's roles, but they simply do not feel that the con-ventional views apply to them, and they express dissatisfaction with the confinements of the role. Few of these women, or in-deed ranching women in the commercial sector, are active in ranch-ing organizations, such as the Texas and Southwestern Cattle Raisers Association. Either they perceive these organizations to be male-oriented or they simply do not have time to participate. There is more organizational participation of women in the pure-bred sector, although this is often in support of husbands, and, as we shall see in chapter 4, there is a great deal of interest and participation among the young women in 4H, FFA, and the junior breed associations.

Although there are commonalities among the contemporary ranching women presented in this chapter, the diversity in their situations and the differences in their characteristics remain more the rule than the exception. In many and important respects, these women and their histories defy categorization and deny no-tions of the "average" or "central tendency." There is important diversity among these ranching women, in their orientations, educations, and "world view." This is the reason for the qualitative approach adopted in the following profiles—to allow the unique-ness of each ranching woman and the differences among them, in their operations and circumstances, to be part of this research.

Angela Bonifazi

"Ranching is not a job; it is a way of life."—Angela Bonifazi

Angela Bonifazi is truly a woman who could inspire legends. After her mother died of a black widow spider bite when Angela was four years old, the girl was adopted by a German couple who had been granted a twelve-hundred-acre tract of land in the rich cotton land along Cedar Greek, a tributary of the Navasota River. Angela was to be their only child. Although Angela was sent away to finishing school, she always returned to the land she loved. At an early age she and her friend Mattie (now Mrs. Mattie Gerke) were cow hands helping with their families' cattle and also with the cattle herds of neighbors—often riding five miles or more to help work cattle.

According to Angela's husband, Albert (who has always worked away from the ranch helping to build many of the beautiful older buildings of Texas A&M University), they were "both raised on horses." Albert also boasts that "Angela is not scared of snakes." As they pull out some pictures from the family album showing six-foot-long rattlesnakes being held at arm's length (sans heads), Angela recounts rather dryly that she has been bitten too many times to be afraid of snakes. She cannot remember the exact number of times she has been bitten—four or five—but is able to physically locate four bites on hands and legs, including on a finger which is deformed since she did not bother going to see the doctor. For snake bite, Angela recommends, "Tie it off and put it in kerosene."

This silver-haired and graceful woman is warmed by the humor of the snake bite stories to the recollection of a time that she was gored and pinned by one of her long-horned cows. Unlike her friend Mattie, Angela does not dehorn her cows, and many have horns that deserve the title "longhorn" although they are not the longhorn breed. With the horn in her side, she held on to the flailing animal until she could get her dogs to distract the animal away from her. After getting off the literal horns of that dilemma, she walked back to the house and asked her granddaughter to "go get her a Band-Aid." Christine Bonifazi remembers the incident quite clearly, commenting that her grandmother had a five-inch wound that was later sutured by the town doctor.

Angela Bonifazi with "Buck"

When I inquired into the reasons why Angela continued and continues to ranch the land she inherited from her adopted parents, she responds that she "couldn't live in town," that "I love it out here," and that "I would die in town." According to her own admissions, backed up by the smiling affirmations of her family and friend Mattie, Angela seldom goes into town at all: "Albert does the grocery shopping"; Angela "only shops at Christmas time."

When she is not taking care of one hundred cows and three bulls, Angela is an avid floriculturalist—even originating some new colors of daylilies and begonias. In this endeavor she has a constant battle with the wildlife on the ranch, particularly the whitetails (deer), which often eat the plants before they can go to seed. Perhaps this explains her one apparent unfulfilled desire. She would like to have a greenhouse in which she could raise her orchids, lilies, and begonias. Other than this, I cannot discern any discontentment underlying the humor and strength of this seventy-three-year-old ranch woman. Even her recent surgery for cancer does not seem a subject of major concern, although because of it she can no longer ride horseback. "Now I ride the truck," she says.

This woman has maintained a working cattle ranch for over half a century – through depressions, recessions, and periods of occasional economic prosperity (1984, the time of this interview, was not such a time for the cattle industry). Through much of this time she has worked the ranch alone. Now she has the help of her five children, although I have the feeling they are unlikely to continue the ranch. According to Angela, none of her sons has ever been very interested in ranch work, preferring their cars and off-ranch activities. Christine, the oldest grandchild, in the eleventh grade, is being trained by her grandmother to "do the cattle." It was Christine who originally wrote to me telling me about her grandmother. Some of her love for the woman and for the ranching heritage are best expressed in her own words:

> As of now my grandmother goes nearly every day to take care of our Santa Gertrudis cattle. She still raises horses and takes care of all her stock. When we bale hay she is out there making sure her "boys", who are grown men and married are doing fine. She still stays with the cattle when they are calving and helps us tag and vaccinate.
>
> My grandmother is truly a woman who has lived a wonderful life in which she has learned much. She understands everything that happens out here. I have learned much from her, as have all of her family.

Christine is, however, uncertain about the future. She wants to go to college at Texas A&M to major in pre-law. Her elders seem to think she will then take her place as the next ranching woman. Her obvious joy in the ranching heritage suggests they might be right. But times are changing even along the banks of the Navasota River. One thousand acres is a large parcel to maintain, particularly with four children as inheritors (including Christine's father). Economically, there have been many poor times for the cattle industry, and new notions of nutrition do not suggest a rising demand. The oil industry that has moved into the Kurten area (the Kurten oil field) has tied up the land but has not distributed much wealth. The Bonifazis have received a total of $175 for their lease of one thousand acres and are suing for release from their lease. Finally, Christine was recently injured in a fall from her horse and has not ridden since the injury. Her love for the lore of her heritage may after all be a respect of the young for the old ways rather than a desire to continue those ways. Christine has the strength of her heritage. She has written the governor to protest the building of a dam that would threaten her land, and she has gotten a response. Her time may simply take her to different acts of courage.

As I look over the vistas of this ranch on the banks of the Navasota River, I am saddened by the thought of impending subdivision—it is surely likely, this close to the growing cities of Bryan and College Station. But I am glad to have seen this land and to have met the women who have tended it.

Jackie Worthington

"If you can't do it right, you might as well sell out."
—Jackie Worthington

In many ways Jackie Worthington represents past, present, and future. She is both a legendary figure from the era of "The All Girl Rodeo" and a modern rancher who is the subject of articles written about her progressive ranch management practices.

Jackie was one of the first women inducted into the National Cowgirl Hall of Fame (1975). She was seven times the world champion bull rider; seven times the cutting horse world champion; and three times the bareback bronc world champion. She sees nothing extraordinary in her accomplishments, telling me "we just did what we had to do at the time." As one of three sisters growing up on a working ranch, and growing up working cattle, riding calves seemed a natural thing to do. As Jackie got bigger, the calves and the challenges simply got bigger, too. She rodeoed for fifteen years, helping to establish the women's circuit for the All Girl Rodeo Association (the GRA) as it developed and flourished during the 1940s and 1950s. Demands were heavy and labor scarce in the cattle industry during the war years. Jackie would return home to help with the ranch until, in 1957, she gave up the circuit to assume responsibilities as owner-manager of the West Fork Ranch. "The ranch needed me and my daddy needed me.

Jackie Worthington, champion bullrider

So I paid the taxes and got some fences put up and bought my first head of cattle."

Dr. O. D. Butler, something of a legend himself around Texas A&M University and in the Charolais cattle business, suggested in an interview (January 30, 1986) that women's extensive, modern-day involvement in the industry occurred as a result of World War II. It was at this time, Dr. Butler feels, that women took over the reins of many Texas ranches, and they never put them down. Although women's extensive involvement cannot be attributed solely to the war, certainly these circumstances may have strengthened ties to the industry which already existed and made it "more acceptable" for women to be cowhands.

In 1986 Jackie still owns and manages eight thousand acres close to Jacksboro, Texas—a land of oil wells and red-tailed hawks, mountain lions, poachers, and grass fires. She runs two hundred straight-bred Angus cows and fifteen purebred Limousin bulls. Her 98 percent calf crop is as uniform a set of commercial cattle as I have ever seen anywhere—sleek and well cared for as they are well bred. Indeed, Jackie's modern ideas about crossbreeding, limited calving seasons, and stringent culling are highly productive management practices. She weans heifer calves that average 556 pounds and steer calves that average 606 pounds. These figures have earned her the notice and regard of the commercial cattle industry.

Jackie Worthington has mechanized her operation to ensure her self-sufficiency. She does everything without help except for palpating her mother cows. However, for all the technical efficiency, Jackie Worthington stays "in touch" with her livestock. She does not use ear tags or any other means of visible identification on her mother cows, but recognizes each one without technical assistance.

It is not easy to adequately describe this woman of the Texas range. She has been a champion bull rider. She has been acknowledged as a progressive in the industry. In 1986, at age sixty-two she is sole manager-operator of eight thousand acres and approximately 350 head of cattle. Her place is superbly organized and full of advantages, including two stocked fish tanks, for the delight of guests and visiting writers. Each shovel, each truck, each sack of feed has a place where it is both accessible and protected; for example, her feed storage areas are rat-proofed. There is no clutter. There is no waste. There is little wanting from this modern cattle ranch as business or as a home.

Jackie remembers the past with affection and pride. Her eyes dance with the recollection of her friends from the rodeo days who are also ranchers. Nancy Binford and Fern Sawyer were both famous rodeo riders during the days of the all-girl rodeos. Jackie still does business with Nancy Binford and her mother, and she stays in touch with Fern Sawyer. Jackie also looks toward the future with courage and sturdy preparation. She is constantly improving her facilities. Yet she maintains the integrity of the differences due to the many stages of development of her ranch and of her self. She has restored the original ranch house. The pens and arenas of her rodeo days are kept operational. These "eras" of her development are represented in tangible form along with the newer additions. Little is left to chance and yet, as with all agricultural and human enterprise, so much remains dependent on it. As one writer describes her: "The land is written all over her face, like some map of life, an indelible record of the

Maurine Godbolt, owner of Clay Mitchell Ranch

spirit of one who lives on the land and knows each crack in the earth. And her ranch is beautiful, kept together and made better for the tenaciousness of this one woman" (Sterber 1986, 42).

Maurine Godbolt

*"I've always resented the fact that just because I was a girl
I couldn't do this or that."* — Maurine Godbolt

Maurine Godbolt sits in a chair next to her new satellite equipment and proclaims her old-fashioned ways. The Clay Mitchell Ranch, with the brand C on the left hip, is six and one-half miles from Marfa and ranges over twenty-nine sections of land (close to thirty square miles). Like most cattle ranchers in the area,

Maurine runs purebred Hereford cattle, crossing only occasionally for milk cows. She usually runs 350 to 400 mother cows, selling off about 300 calves a year. Maurine shipped earlier than others this year in September, before the antelope season. There will be extensive antelope hunting this year as well as an antelope roundup to ship the surplus to Arizona instead of killing them—a plan that Maurine supports.

Under the pressure of questioning, Maurine says that her family (her mother) came to the area before the turn of the century. However, Maurine has no fondness for history. In her own words, "I couldn't stand what had happened before, I just wanted to know what would happen next." She is more kindly disposed to recent events, such as the filming of a movie called *High Lonesome* (starring John Barrymore, Jr.) at the ranch house during her father's time.

Some probing reveals that the Mitchells settled in Antelope Springs in the late 1800s and branched out from there. Maurine's mother came out from Mississippi to teach school and stayed to marry Clay Mitchell, Maurine's father. Maurine is their only child. She assumed control of the ranch in 1955 after her father died. She and her mother decided that they did not want to lease the ranch, in spite of considerable pressure to do so. At this time, Maurine began to implement some new production practices such as putting the bulls up so that calves would be born only at certain times of the year, rather than all year round. Even in those early days young Maurine sought the counsel of very few, saying she preferred making her own mistakes to the confusion of other people's opinions. She likes "to work my cattle slow," with the help of one hand. She doesn't like to run her cows or lose track of her animals. She keeps a running inventory of each of her pastures. Her pride and affection for her Hereford cattle punctuate her descriptions and her procedures, including expensive, and economically unprofitable, Caesarean sections for animals that have difficulties calving.

The slow drawl of this West Texas woman is camouflage for a quick wit and considerable education. Few know that she has a degree in chemistry from Duke University. She also has some commercial training and is presently taking a course in computers to aid her in cattle management. In this she reflects the forward look of the progressive cattle breeder, even as she also rep-

Clay Mitchell Ranch—where the antelope play

resents the traditional commitment to the Hereford cattle of the West Texas cattle industry.

At sixty-three, fiercely independent, Maurine lives on the land where she grew up, land her grandfather sold her father. She bounces over the rutted and pitted dirt roads of her ranch in a blue pickup. She chain smokes Tarletons and carries boxes of them in the pockets of her plaid shirt as she points with pride to her cattle and her land and tersely describes a way of life she does not expect will long endure.

After high school Maurine went to North Carolina to attend Duke University—"to get as far away" as she could from people who knew and cared too much about other people's business. She majored in chemistry, not because she thought she would become a chemist, but because that is what she was interested in. "Girls had no future" back then—"we were just supposed to get married," she says. In the 1940s Maurine did marry—a man who now owns the local feed store. She divorced a few years later and moved "back home" to her ranch. "I wasn't cut out to be married," she says. "Marriage was boring to me."

Since 1955, the year of her father's death, Maurine has run the ranch. Increasingly, she has run the ranch her way, incorporating new and modern techniques that many of her neighbors, as well as her father, would not consider traditional or right. She has managed well. The Mitchell Ranch is one of the area's few old ranches that remain undivided and prosperous—where "you can see forever" and watch the antelope play.

Ethel Williams

"Don't think I don't do it all, because I do."—Ethel Williams

Ethel Nelson Williams ranches the land once ruled by Shanghai Pierce, cattle baron and founder of the modern Texas Brahman herds, in the Coastal Bend country of Matagorda County, bordered by the Gulf of Mexico. She daily drives the sixty miles from Bay City to Collegeport, where she tends to her herd of fifty crossbred mother cows and two registered Brahman bulls on the Nelson Ranch of "a little less than a thousand acres." In this land of alligators, coyotes, and bobcats (I have a picture of the bobcat Mrs. Williams shot), Ethel Williams runs her cows on approximately one-half of the acreage, which also contains the original ranch house, the Collegeport Cemetery, and 450 acres of salt grass. The salt grass is truly pasture land—it cannot be planted for row crops—but cattle do well on it, particularly when it is "tenderized by being burned off every other year." Ethel also plants forty acres of hay every year. Her sister farms the rest of the acreage.

Ethel considers her ranching to be "a hobby" since she became a widow in 1978. It is also an important and daily part of her life—the part which often gives solace and meaning as well as income to this woman who has traveled the world and lived in places as distant as Tripoli. She was living in Tripoli when her husband died. Now, according to her sister, "Ethel has taken the family ranch over and enjoys the country life and ranching."

Ethel Adell Nelson was born in Bay City on June 4, 1923, the second of two daughters. Her folks came from Kansas in the first decade of the century after hearing of "the Texas land rush and of the Burton D. Hurd Land Co. excursions to Collegeport, where the artesian wells flowed excessively, citrus fruit, bountiful corn crops, and wonderful garden truck farms could be raised and luscious berries grew wild." Although Ethel's father appears to have had a successful business as a veterinarian for large Clydesdale horses in Kansas, the lure of this Texas land was too strong to resist. The family moved to Collegeport, where her father became a tick inspector for Matagorda County. A picture of her dad shows one of the early Brahman bulls in the area. Her mother lived to ninety-one and her father to age eighty-nine. Her mother was a country girl who "rode and was a tremendous asset." Her mother drove and helped with the cows until she was eighty-nine, when she was finally persuaded to give up driving.

Except for actual transport of the calves to market, Ethel now does all work with the cattle without help. She prefers to handle her cattle herself, because she considers most of the available help to be unduly rough and upsetting to the cows—cows that follow her across the pasture and eat from her hand. Ethel acknowledges that "when you get them in the pens they are dangerous." She will not work them in the pens with men who come to haul the calves to market because "the men will get them too excited with all their screaming, yelling, and hollering," and "you just don't know what is going on behind you." Williams says her cows are now afraid of men on horseback, and she can take them into the pens much easier with her pickup truck just "riding along and talking to them." She walks easily up to the biggest bull, which weighs in excess of twenty-five hundred pounds. "Don't think I don't do it all, because I do."

When I ask about her daily tasks, Ethel responds with a low laugh, almost a chuckle, that her days are really very filled. Yet there is an undercurrent of loneliness in her life: she was married for forty-one years, and has been widowed for six. With her cattle she is self-sufficient and complete. In referring to the concern, indeed the disquietude of her family about her ranching activities (she gave up horseback riding for their sake), Ethel says, "I am comfortable, but no one else is!"

In the intervening six and one-half years since her husband's death, Ethel has developed the ranch considerably—putting the full force of a tremendous energy and vitality into improving the herd and the ranch. She acknowledges few limitations—carpentry

Ethel Williams introducing her cows

among them—but for the most part, she fixes the fences, clears the brush, hauls the hay alone. She feeds two pickup loads of twenty-four bales of hay three times a week. When the weather is bad she feeds every evening. Last winter (1985), during the long freeze, Ethel hauled water to the cows in garbage cans when the tank and wells froze over.

I ask her about the future as I have asked about the past. Ethel feels that the nuclear power industry, with its tremendous land requirements, poses the biggest threat to the commercial cattle industry in Matagorda County, along with the growth of resorts which also compete for the land. The stocking rates (the number of cows per acre) cannot be high in a land that hovers between hurricanes and drought.

In the past Ethel taught school, with special interest in special children. She helped raise money to build a special school for re-tarded children in Matagorda County. She has also been a social worker. She has served on numerous community boards, including the Matagorda Council for Retarded Children, the Garden Club, and the United Fund. She plays the piano and the organ and "loves to cook." She has two daughters and an adored grandchild.

Martha Ann Clement Lawhorn

Selling out is not an option.

Martha Ann Clement Lawhorn represents the third generation of a ranching family. She intends for La Vista to survive for at least one more generation. Martha Ann has made legal preparation that the ranch not be sold by her two daughters, one of whom presently lives on the ranch with her husband (and, I feel, is expected to assume eventual control of the ranch). This daughter, Kimberly, provides the potential for the fourth and fifth generations, one more of which will be a woman.

Martha Ann's partnership with husband Floyd Lawhorn is lucrative for both. Since Floyd owns an eleven hundred–acre ranch in Bell County, they are able to share the costs and the chores of some heavy (and very expensive) equipment. Martha Ann took us for "a drive" in one of their 350 horsepower tractors, which is used exclusively for producing hay. After some comparative shopping, Martha Ann had paid $64,000 for this piece of equipment, now shared between the two ranches, giving each access to an efficient and expensive piece of ranch equipment. To my surprise, Martha Ann says that she can plow 250 acres on less than a tank of gas.

When she was ranching with her mother, most of the tasks and decisions concerning La Vista were performed and made by Martha Ann. She bought the equipment, baled the hay, laid the irrigation pipe, sold the cows, and decided when to buy replacements, usually young cows with calves at side. She still does most of these things, as well as many others considered the usual purview of men, such as pesticide application. Now, as partners, she and Floyd share many tasks and decisions as they share equipment, although each appears to be the majority voter for his or her own ranch. Martha Ann keeps the books for both ranches, and Floyd does the planting for both. Cultivation is another matter. Martha Ann does the baling—usually five hundred of the big

The tractor Martha Ann Lawhorn uses for the hay she grows

round bales (because of the drought in 1984, she expects to bale
only two hundred).

She has, in the past, helped to bale hay on neighbors' ranches
in exchange for some more hay, but in the year I interview her
the drought is so bad that she will have to buy additional hay
or sell off some of her cows, a choice faced by her neighbors as
well. There is no surplus for exchange this year.

Despite the constant challenges of weather – which many would
define as hardships – the thought of selling land is anathema to
Martha Ann. Although twice married, Martha Ann has never
lived off the ranch. Through times of drought and flood and uni-
versally tough economic times for cattle ranchers, Martha Ann
has fought to keep her land. She does not see her ranch in terms
of acres, but as her home, a whole, a totality. And this whole
is sacrosanct. She is now using much of the profit from cows and
wheat to buy up her sister's share of the ranch. Her sister wanted
to sell, which gave Martha Ann no choice: the ranch will not
be divided. Selling out is not an option for Martha Ann. It is
a sin.

The 125 mother cows, mostly cross-bred, are not dehorned. Martha Ann feels they have the right to protect themselves and their young. In this country, that need is more than myth. It encompasses predators such as coyotes, wild dogs, and mountain lions. The six bulls are purebred: Beefmaster, Charolais, and Brahman. Buying the more expensive purebred bulls to use with cross-bred cows is a practice of many commercial cow-calf breeders. The intent is to get large, range-rugged, and nutrition-efficient young that will grow quickly and bring top price on a minimum of supplement (additional feed over and above grass and hay). Calves are usually sold in March. In 1984 some of the five-hundred-pound calves sold for $300 each.

I asked, "What kind of education is best for ranching?" I was told that one "is born to ranching." Ranching would thus appear to be more an inherited status than one achieved through any process of education. This relationship of the women to their land is indeed inherited—passed down from generation to generation—sometimes, as in the case of La Vista, from father and mother to daughter. Sometimes the process of inheritance skips a generation and passes from grandmother to granddaughter (as may be the case for the Bonifazi Ranch).

While being born on a ranch could be a necessary condition for ranching, it is far from a sufficient one. This life appears to select only the very strong. Few would survive—much less relish or cherish—this way of living. Like Angela Bonifazi, Martha Ann Clement Lawhorn is amused by situations and constant conditions of ranch life that would strike terror in the hearts of most of us: rattlesnakes so big that their trails look like the single track of a large tractor; floods that come in the middle of the night and require swimming to help the cows instead of escape; droughts that wizen the land into desert and bring winter landscapes into the midst of summer.

With the help of hired hands, Martha Ann ranched this land with her father, then for her mother, then alone. She ranches now with Floyd. There is relative prosperity. The ranch has always paid for itself and has made a profit for Martha Ann as for her father. There is relative tranquility. Peacocks roam the green yard of the ranch house, the only green in a year of drought. A tame yearling deer, named Buckshot, rests in an enclosure with tame turkey and wild mallard ducks, all free to leave at any time as the enclosure is not topped. A gaggle of twenty to thirty geese

Long-horned mother cow and cross-bred calf

walk along the perimeter of the water tank. All of these views are part of La Vista—the many views of this ranch.

I have the feeling that times are a little easier now, not necessarily better, but with a little more time and a little more money to use as leisure rather than to give back to the ranch. Now there are trips to Ruidoso and to Laredo, Martha Ann's favorite place, in the big king-cab pickup truck that has been converted to run off butane. There is time for planning and for talking as well as doing. I am invited to come back for roundup in the early spring.

A Qualitative Summary

There are some notable similarities among the ranching women interviewed for this research. All of the women were provided the opportunity to be ranchers through inheritance. Most of these women also were socialized to ranch work. Usually in the absence of male siblings, they grew up doing ranch chores. Most identify strong father and mother figures. They all originated from intact families. In terms of personal characteristics, these women appear to share a passion for the land that exceeds the power of economics to explain. They are ranch operators and managers as well as ranch owners. They are successful, making money and holding on to the land when many around them are being forced out by drought or flood, high taxes, high interest, high costs of equipment and supplies, encroaching urbanization, lack of support, and poor health. They are not optimistic about the future of ranching, yet they continue to battle to maintain their ranches in the face of tremendous adversity. Courage and independence and tenacity are shared by these women. They are "tough customers," worthy of legends. Perhaps, against the odds of economics, which favors the large operations, and culture, which favors males as cattlemen and ranchers, these women will retain their ranches through the 1990s. The probabilities are against continuation. However, in three cases, there are daughters and granddaughters who could inherit and keep the land for yet another generation of ranching women.

4

A Changing Industry

The hallowed occupation of rancher is rich with tradition. However, it is not an occupation with much growth potential. Opportunities to be a rancher, particularly in the old style, are rather narrow and circumscribed by circumstances of birth. For most of the ranching women interviewed in the course of this research, and all of those presented in chapter 3, ranching is an inherited occupation. Moreover, coming from a ranching background does not guarantee an opportunity to be a rancher.

Ranching is a constricting occupation, meaning that there are fewer opportunities to be a rancher today than a generation ago. Indeed, there are very few full-time ranching opportunities today. Most ranching operations are subsidized by outside "off-farm" income. There are more people feeding cattle in Texas today through off-farm employment than was true in the 1950s, the 1960s, or even the 1970s. In addition, the opportunities to be a rancher are, for women, limited by other considerations. For a woman to inherit a ranch, she is likely to have no or only female siblings. This reflects the cultural selection of male children as ranchers when male children are available. Furthermore, the women who have "chosen" ranching see their roles as unusual, although not necessarily as "deviant." They tend to be strongly independent in their views and in their recognition of themselves as ranchers, maintaining a heritage that even they do not feel can long endure.

This chapter begins with the profile of a woman who maintains her ties to a ranching heritage in Clay County while she practices law in Brazos County. Her name is Angela Neville.

A Ranching Heritage and a Professional Career:
Angela Neville

Angela Neville represents the fourth generation of a ranching family. She is also a graduate of the University of Texas Law School and is a practicing attorney in Bryan, Texas. Angela raises beef cattle in partnership with her father near Henrietta, Texas, in Clay County, twenty-five miles from the Oklahoma border—a land of hot temperatures in the summer (105° to 110°) and cold in the winter. Angela's father, who is sixty-six, runs 120 head of cows on two thousand acres. Of this acreage, Angela's father and mother own eleven hundred acres, with another nine hundred acres in trust for Angela and her brother and sister, placed there by Angela's grandmother. All of the children in this generation have retained some ties to the cattle industry and the land of their heritage, although each now pursues an off-farm career. With "the wild fluctuations in cattle prices," Angela feels that very few can make it in full-time ranching. Because of the volatility of the cattle market and other noneconomic factors, Angela may well typify the Texas beef cattle rancher of the future: A man or woman who owns relatively few cattle (the majority of beef operations in Texas run fewer than fifty head, and 37 percent have less than twenty head) and who pursues a full-time nonfarm career. Hence, these modern "ranchers" retain strong ties to a heritage and an industry while earning a living elsewhere. Retirement may bring them home again to the range on a full-time basis.

Although Angela is a six-hour drive from her cows, she keeps up with cattle markets and also with animal health news, a subject she finds particularly interesting. On her frequent visits home she likes to get out in the pasture and look over her cows. She notes that "they are interesting animals in the way they react to weather situations and interact with each other." Cows are also strongly protective toward their offspring—a characteristic Angela much admires, as an attorney who sees many spouse and child abuse cases. Angela registered her brand in 1984 as the N. Her brother, an accountant in Wichita Falls, uses the same brand as her grandfather. Her sister has not registered a brand but is active in the Cow Belles, an "auxiliary" association of the Texas and Southwestern Cattle Raisers Association, which is largely responsible for consumer information about the beef industry. What the future holds in the way of continuation of the ranch, no one

Angela Neville feeding her cows

knows. Angela feels that her brother would like to go into full-time ranching, but with a family of three small children, "they could not make it." It would also be difficult for Angela to practice law in Henrietta, a town of three thousand, with three lawyers already in residence. As we have talked over time, I have sensed that Angela is thinking more about the prospects of setting up practice closer to her land in one of the nearby major metropolitan areas such as Wichita Falls. Thirty-two and single, Angela may indeed be the strongest force for the continuation of the Neville Ranch. She is keenly interested in the preservation of the land—an attribute she shares with most ranching women—sometimes disagreeing with her sister and brother about "stocking rates," the ratio of cows to acreage, which she feels could damage the long-term fertility of the land.

As a hobby, when her busy schedule as a court lawyer serving several counties allows time off, Angela is a patron of the arts, in particular, the performing arts. Angela serves on the board of directors for the Navasota Theater Alliance, in a historic and newly renovated cultural area near Bryan. She is also a member of an association of Volunteer Lawyers and Accountants for the Arts, and does free legal tasks for the performing arts. From a youth who "fed out steer calves to save money for college" to a dynamic young woman who serves both the judicial community and the arts, and who retains strong ties to her ranching heritage with particular interests in herd health and nutrition, Angela represents a diversity of interests and a strong personal drive that could be essential for the continuation of the Texas cattle industry in the twenty-first century.

Women in the Sale Barn and the Show Ring

There are approximately 150 state-inspected livestock auction markets or sale barns in the state of Texas. In 1984 these markets processed 7.7 million head of cattle.[1]

Near Interstate highway 35, connecting Austin with Dallas and Fort Worth, is one of the most profitable and attractive commercial auction facilities in the state. The facility is owned, operated, and managed by Mrs. Adele Uptmore. Located in the town of West, West Auction, Inc., holds a weekly commercial sale every Thursday at 12:30 P.M., with other special sales on Saturday. Mrs. Uptmore also serves as a general manager for purebred auctions.

This is a very attractive facility—above the norm for commercial auction barns—with ceiling fans and a sign that says, "If you spit on your floor at home feel free to spit on this one," aimed at the smokeless tobacco users. The floors and the wood paneling on the walls are clean and shining. There is no tobacco juice in evidence.

Adele Uptmore doesn't define many things as a crisis. Someone bringing in cows at the last moment before auction does little to disturb her serenity, nor does my arrival and interview on sale day. She is a lovely woman, in the Hollywood sense of lovely, who has raised five children, four of whom have graduated from Texas A&M University. The last son, Brian, is most interested in cattle. He is a high school senior and also plans to attend Texas A&M.

Adele began in the auction barn business in 1980. Before she

Adele Uptmore in front of her auction barn

bought it, the business had failed three times. Adele was looking for a challenge to compare with the challenge of raising five children. She says this does not compare! The failing auction barn did present a challenge, though. Six years after she bought it, in a time of industry truncation and economic malaise, West Auction was grossing $11 million a year. Half of this amount is returned to the local economy.

Adele has about twenty-five people working for her. She seems able to coordinate them with a minimum of adrenaline flowing and is continuously gracious and serene—in no way distracted from the work of the day, to sell about 750 head of cattle along with some hogs and horses.

In about 1970 Adele became very ill and was diagnosed with multiple sclerosis. The diagnosis was wrong, but "it took me three to four years to come out of it and, after physically being all right, to psychologically become healthy again." One of the ways Adele regained her mental health was to read extensively in psychology. She now uses this informal education in psychology to run a successful business. She also used it in raising her five children.

Adele Uptmore at work during an auction

Another woman who manages sales and, in addition, raises purebred longhorn cattle is Mrs. Betty Lamb of Somerville, Texas. On the day of her sale in 1987 I was able to obtain photographs of her in various roles, which included successfully "coaxing" a cow with six-foot horns back into the chute.

Also self-employed, Cindy Warnke Walls started out showing cows and helping her daddy, manager of an Angus cattle operation, at the age of nine. At the age of thirty-three Cindy is owner, manager, and chief worker of Warnke Cattle Service headquartered in La Coste, Texas. Warnke Cattle Service is a highly specialized cattle "fitting" service, which supplies customized grooming, trimming, clipping, hauling, and show training for cows on the show circuit (Cindy's first love) and for cattle for sale at the prestigious and expensive events held in hotel ballrooms, such as the Shamrock Hilton in Houston and La Mansion in Austin. Some of these sales are "black tie" affairs.

Although the money tends to be better in fitting cows for sale, Cindy prefers the show circuit—the sequence of major cattle shows

Adele Uptmore with a customer

beginning in the fall and continuing through the winter and spring in places like Denver, Fort Worth, Houston, and San Antonio. This season, 1984, Cindy, with the help of one or two workers, will manage twenty-five head of cattle, including two-thousand-pound bulls, through the show season. She will take some of her charges as far away as Denver and will stay with them for the duration of the show (nine days for the Denver show). The work is not for the average person.

Cindy says that for the Brenham show in October, 1984, she took eighteen head. Over the five nights of the show she managed to get nine hours of sleep. Her days often start at 4:00 or 5:00 A.M. and last until midnight. And the work is not only long but arduous: washing, grooming, clipping, trimming, and soothing the often irascible half-ton heifers and three-quarter-ton bull calves. Even the tails of the heifers and bulls must be "balled" for the shows—that is, washed, combed, teased, sprayed, and curled back into a fluffy ball. Keeping the cows fed, clean, healthy, and out of trouble requires patience and strength possessed by few. The work must be done, she says, when "it's cold and nasty" (few

Betty Lamb at her Longhorn sale

of the show cattle facilities are heated) and when "it's hot with flies." The flies around cows in hot weather can be fearsome. Through it all, Cindy loves the cattle fitting business, which she entered in 1969. First working for someone else, the large cattle company Rio Vista International, which employed her mother and later her father, she now works for herself.

She tells me that she really started her own business because "everyone told me I couldn't do it." When she started, there were "no other women on the road then and they [the men] made it pretty tough." There were "lots of snide remarks and skeptics who said 'you're a girl and you can't do it.'" Cindy remembers her reply: "'Stand back and watch!' They made fun of me, but I had lots of cows, and they finally decided I was there for a reason—to work and to win." Now, a decade later, Cindy is still very evident as one of the most successful cattle fitters in the industry. She is still working very hard and still winning shows. She still

Cindy Warnke at Houston

helps to bring in large sums of money for the sale cattle (some would say the most important shows of all—where the money is made). But she is no longer the only woman on the circuit or fitting the cattle for sales. According to Cindy, "most of the fitters now hire women because they know we can do a good job." However, through the years of my research and participation in the purebred cattle business, I have observed only one other young woman try to "go it alone" in the fitting business. At times she has worked for Warnke Cattle Fitters and at times for LaRue Douglas, who for many years has been the largest fitter for Brahman and Brahman-influence cattle.

In July, 1986, under the hot Texas sun near Georgetown (in the Austin area off IH 35), fifty-seven students, ages eight to forty-five, undertook a grueling four-day course on fitting and showing purebred Brahman and Brahman-influence cattle. These are students of the LaRue Douglas cattle fitting school. In this, the twentieth session offered over a span of ten years, 50 percent of the participants are women and girls.

Cattle showing is a demanding and fairly exact "science" re-

Class 1 of the LaRue Douglas Cattle Fitting School, including eight-year-
old Beba

quiring knowledge, stamina, and savvy of both cattle and people.
In order to compete, one must learn how to halter break cattle,
feed them properly, trim and clip them to certain specifications
(and always to individual advantage), and show according to pre-
scribed rules of performance for cow and handler. Strapping men
have been known to wilt in the shade, which is about ninety-five
degrees in Georgetown, Texas, in July. Pulling around a thousand-
pound heifer or "ton of bull" is no easy job (cows do not lead
naturally), and the task is complicated by the behavior of the other
cows and by the requirements of the competition to walk and
stand in particular ways, while always trying to make the animal
show to best advantage.

On the last day of the four-day session I observed students of
the LaRue School participating in a simulated cattle show, complete with outside judges and competitions for the best showmanship and cattle judging abilities. There were three classes, distinguished by the ages of the fifty-seven students. Although there
is no way to replicate the heat and the dust and the tension of

Hard-working teens in class 2 of the LaRue Douglas Cattle Fitting School

competition, the pictures I took provide some insight to the presence and determination of the female students, including eight-year-old Beba (in class 1) and her mother (in class 3).

Women in Herd Health and Reproductive Technology

The representation of women in the supporting, auxiliary categories of the beef cattle industry has grown with the development of these divisions. Two such areas are herd health and reproductive technology. A growing demand for modern herd health practices has drawn an increasing number of women into the ranks of large animal veterinary medicine. Palpation, artificial insemination (AI), and brucellosis testing are necessary herd health practices, not necessarily limited to the veterinary practitioner (except for brucellosis testing and health papers), but often provided by the large animal doctor at low cost. For example, the cost of palpation is usually one or two dollars a cow. I have known one herd health veterinarian, Dr. Marla Hendricks, profiled below, to palpate a hundred cows in an afternoon after working all morn-

Beba's mother (second from left) and other adults of class 3, LaRue Douglas Cattle Fitting School

ing in a small animal clinic. Although women are increasingly visible in the profession of veterinary medicine, making up almost 50 percent of students in veterinary schools, and about as likely as men to choose food animal medicine, they are even more visible in the support services of reproductive laboratories. These laboratories specialize in the collection, freezing, and storage of bull semen and in the production of frozen embryos from donor cows. One such "bull stud" is described below. It is part of Granada Corporation, owned and managed by the Ellers family (David Ellers was also chairman of the Board of Regents of Texas A&M during this period), and among the largest vertically integrated beef cattle producers in the United States. They also have facilities in England and South America and compete in the manufacture of turkeys an shrimp as well as in the production of Brangus and Simbrah cattle.

A Bull Stud

Granada Sire Services processes semen of two hundred bulls a year and stores four hundred thousand units of semen. It is one

Becky Everette at Granada Sire Services, shown with inventory control and other equipment

of the largest and most modern "bull studs" in Central Texas. Six of the eleven employees of Granada Sire Services, a part of Granada, Inc., are women. One of these women is Becky Everette, whose job is titled laboratory coordinator. Becky has been with Granada Sire Services since it opened. She is responsible for semen evaluation and quality control. Originally from North Carolina, Becky holds a degree in animal science. She worked for Medina Valley Laboratories in Castroville, Texas, for almost two years before hearing of the opening with Granada in Wheelock. At Granada Sire Services she and her daughter, aged eleven months, are frequently the guides for visitors to the semen-processing part of the bull stud. Another woman, Susan Amick, a Texas A&M graduate in animal science, is in charge of semen shipments. Each of the large semen storage tanks at Granada holds

Susan Amick with some of the large semen storage tanks, Granada Sire Services

seventy thousand doses of semen. The tanks contain liquid nitrogen, which keeps the semen frozen to a temperature of −320°F. Premature thawing of the semen, once frozen, would kill the sperm cells. The straws (doses) of semen must be processed and handled expertly and efficiently. Deposits must be evaluated for quality and recorded with meticulous care. Withdrawals must also be carefully prepared for shipment in special nitrogen-filled containers and recorded. In addition, each bull in the stud must undergo constant health testing. In a normal season, between October 1 and June 1, each bull in the stud will undergo two collections per week, yielding on average one thousand units of semen to be processed.

All of this semen is collected and frozen for one reason: so that the genetic material of a single bull can be used for literally thousands of cows, whereas the average bull can fertilize only twenty to forty cows a season through natural insemination. A bull's fertility actually depends upon a number of environmental and physiological factors, which are all routinely "controlled" in a stud. No bull has been known to break his leg while being collected, although many prize bulls have been lost to accidents in the pasture. Therefore, in addition to the expanded genetic potential, bull studs also offer sheltered environments for favored and very expensive bulls. In the middle 1980s several bulls were valued at a million dollars each.[2] Of course, with all this semen, there must be a constant effort to market the product and train commercial as well as purebred breeders to the advantages of artificial insemination (AI), the process where frozen semen is artificially deposited into the reproductive tract of a cow. The industry of frozen semen depends upon the use of artificial insemination, and the success of the technique depends upon the skill of AI technicians. These technicians, who are often cattle raisers seeking to do their own AI work, are trained in regular and regulated AI schools.

AI School
On a hot day in August, 1986, three instructors and twenty-three "students," including me, began a week of classes in herd health and the techniques of artificial insemination (AI) and pregnancy detection (palpation). The course was sponsored by the American Breeders Service (ABS) with guest speakers from the Extension Service of Texas A&M. Five of the participants were women. Kathryn Cole was present as one of the instructors in charge of AI procedure, specifically, preparation and handling of the semen before insertion. She and her husband, Don Cole, travel over a five-state area conducting these courses. Don Cole is obviously the "chief" organizer, and Kathryn is unpaid for her work. Kathryn Cole also handles most of the bookkeeping for the course, including keeping records of which students have successfully completed which tasks toward certification, as well as inventories of the educational materials and of sales (ABS sells AI equipment as well as semen). Based in Fort Worth, Kathryn has participated in these courses for the past two years, and I do not see from my observations how the course could be completed without her instruction. Nevertheless, she works on a "volunteer" and unpaid basis.

Lisa Gerhart participated in the course as a student, learning

Kathryn Cole instructing students in proper semen-handling procedures at AI School. At right is student Sally Allison.

primarily the techniques of AI. Lisa is co-owner of one of the largest Bralers ranches in the state, running sixty-five head of breeding age females on 360 areas in Giddings. Her husband, Gary, is president of the state association for this new breed of cattle — crossing Salers with Brahman. They do have a ranch manager, who had taken the ABS course earlier, but Lisa wants to be a more active participant in their AI program. She and husband Gary have two sons, ages two and a half and four and a half. Raised on a ranch in Oklahoma, Lisa met Gary while both were students at the University of Texas. During the times I have observed Lisa subsequent to the school, for example at cattle sales and the Houston Livestock Show, her husband Gary presents the perfect image of a banker, complete with three-piece suits, while Lisa most often appears in jeans and well-worn boots and, obviously, has been handling the cattle (boots do not lie).

Sally Allison was registered for both the AI and palpation segments of the course and intends to do all the "clean up" work on her American Gray Brahman ranch (meaning, she breeds by AI all the cows not bred by their herd sire). Now in her early forties, Sally Allison has been breeding commercial cattle in Texas since 1969. In 1979 she and her family began breeding purebred Brahman, led into the purebred industry by the eldest daughter, Michelle. Michelle was in the ninth grade when she decided she wanted to show calves as an FFA project. As a result of her daughter's interest in showing, Sally bought a "nice looking little Brahman heifer" at the sale barn and bred the heifer, by AI, to a very good Manso bull. From that mating, they produced their first show-ring champion. At this point Sally's husband also became interested in the showing aspect of the purebred cattle business, and the family became full-fledged purebred breeders.

Robin Sibley, whom I met again when she was working for Cindy Warnke and LaRue Douglas Cattle Fitters, was also registered for both AI and palpation during the ABS school. An animal science major at Texas A&M University, Robin wanted to go on to A&M's graduate school of veterinary medicine. However, money is a problem, and her grades must be very high for vet school. Now in her early twenties, Robin is looking for a way to finish her undergraduate degree at Texas A&M and wants to find a job working with cattle. Robin has two older sisters, neither of whom shares her interest in agriculture.[3]

These three students, Lisa, Sally, and Robin, were full participants in every aspect of the course. The only activity they (and most of the men) did not participate in was actually running the cows into the stalls. This extracurricular "event" was dominated by three men with extensive cattle handling experience. There were no pet cows in this bunch. However, all of the women and most of the men participated in moving and assembling the heavy cattle panels, which served as stalls for the actual AI work. Indeed, it was my perception that the three women students were by far the most serious and most interested in the various phases and requirements of the course, compared with most of the males, particularly the younger males, who tended to treat AI as something of a joke (the procedure involves inserting a steel "syringe" into the vagina of the cow and through the cartilage opening to the uterus). The women seemed intensely interested in both the principles and the practice of the modern herd management tool of AI and palpation, and with one exception (me), none seemed offended by the blood, gore, and manure, which often reached beyond the plastic shoulder sleeves of the aspiring AI technicians. All passed the requirements for certification.

Herd Health Medicine

On July 4, 1987, we were working cattle for Grassburr Cattle Partners, near Bryan, Texas. After four hours of rounding up cows, drawing blood for brucellosis tests, giving injections of Ivomec, palpating for pregnancy, obtaining weights, and tattooing calves, Dr. Marla Hendricks and I sat down to conclude the official portion of an interview for an observation begun two years ago.

I first "discovered" Dr. Hendricks as a herd health veterinarian in an announcement for a sale of registered Beefmaster cattle. She was listed as the "sale veterinarian" and she was also a consignor. Marla and her husband were selling cattle in the sale. I attended to find out more about Dr. Hendricks. The following week I called her to introduce myself as a fellow cattle breeder interested in herd health procedures. That was in the spring of 1986. Two years later, I had a certified brucellosis-free herd and a tremendous admiration for my herd veterinarian, Marla Hendricks, D.V.M.

Dr. Henricks practices in both small animal and large animal medicine. She practices "companion animal medicine" in an in-town veterinary clinic during the day, and in the evenings, on weekends, and on holidays she practices "food animal" and equine medicine, providing both routine health and emergency services to cattle and horses in Brazos County. This is where producers feel the greatest need, according to Dr. Hendricks, "when they are in a crisis, that is when they want a veterinarian."

The emergency treatment of large animals is where Dr. Hendricks perceives the greatest demand for her services. While she enjoys herd health and perceives this to be the goal for planned health procedures, much of her practice consists of going to farms to handle emergencies—cows with calving problems, horses that have cut-up feet. I have seen her work in all kinds of environmental conditions: at 10:00 p.m. in subfreezing January temperatures using flashlights to see as she flushes the womb of a cow with a retained placenta; at 12:00 noon in 102° of swirling, manure-choked heat and dust as she vaccinates seventeen-hundred-pound cows against the myriad diseases and parasites that pester and

Marla Hendrick, D.V.M.

kill cattle in this humid river-bottom land where she practices
medicine.

Born in Arkansas, the youngest of four girls born to "older
than average" parents, Marla Hendricks feels her most significant
agricultural experience came from working on a hundred-acre truck
farm when she was fifteen. The farm, belonging to her mother's
cousin, ran about thirty cows in addition to raising produce. Here
she gained her insight into the needs of the small agricultural producer and discovered her own enjoyment of farm life.

In 1974 Marla came to Texas A&M University to study wildlife and fisheries science. She graduated with a B.S. degree and
went on to Washington State to pursue research begun in her senior
year at A&M. She returned to Texas A&M as a graduate student
in bioengineering. In the process, she gained a background in
mathematics and computers, which she uses in her herd health
practice. However, she "always had a desire to get back into doing
something practical" that she could be "very happy with." With
her background in mathematics and computers, Marla could easily

have chosen a research career, but for her, "the practical aspects of veterinary medicine were much more rewarding." She obtained her D.V.M. degree in 1985.

Marla works an average eighteen-hour day. During the years I have known her, she has never failed in the diagnosis or treatment of a herd problem. She says, "The most rewarding thing, the thing that constantly renews you, is the cow with the calving problems, that thing you accomplish and that makes a difference that you have done it."

Women in Agricultural Communication and Information Services

In 1972, Texas A&M University graduated its first woman majoring in agricultural journalism. By 1979 women had become a majority of those with agricultural journalism majors. Today there are almost four times as many women as men in this program. Many of these young women are members of a student professional association, the Ag Communicators of Tomorrow. In November, 1986, I talked with several of these young women, and one young man, about their backgrounds, their decisions to become ag journalists, and the future of the beef cattle industry.

Agricultural Journalism
In large part, these young women come to Texas A&M from agricultural backgrounds and have well-defined career goals. For some this program is a means of entering other agricultural careers. In the words of one: "I used my ag journalism background as a stepping stone into a master's program in ag economics. I plan to work for the Foreign Agricultural Service as an agricultural attaché. As an attaché, I will be required to write reports from various embassies on the various countries' agricultural situations. Eventually I plan to work as a trade negotiator for the U.S.T.R."

Another, a young woman from Lexington, Texas, has been on Cow Belles scholarship for two years.[4] She "grew up on a family ranch," raising commercial cattle with three hundred mother cows. Her father and mother are both full-time ranchers, and she is the eldest of three children. The ranch has been in the family for fifty years. She comments: "Ag journalism offered the 'best of both worlds.' Combined my love of writing and agriculture.

Plus [it] gave me a chance to work with the type of people I know and respect the most."

A third young woman, Belinda Hood, president of the association when I spoke with her, writes:

> Until I was seven years old my father worked for ———— Airlines. When he got the opportunity to buy my grandfather's purebred Santa Gertrudis ranch, he grabbed it because that was his life-long dream. For fourteen years I've worked with cattle. Showed in the ring, fed, branded, vaccinated, castrated, etc. I've also been stomped more times than I care to remember. I am also a certified A.I. technician.

With regard to her choice of a career, Ms. Hood says: "After talking to many people in the cattle industry, I realized my best opportunity in agriculture would be to combine communications and agriculture in my career. Having an ag background, I wanted to be involved in agriculture and I feel my best opportunity is in that field." There seemed to be some consensus among the members of this group that agricultural journalism offered the "best opportunity for women" of the agricultural majors—that they would face less discrimination because of gender.

Although many of these students had extensive agricultural experience, this was not true in all cases. One of the young women, now a senior, "grew up in a suburb of Houston" with virtually no agricultural experience: "My grandfather taught agronomy at A&M. I decided to get to know my heritage by taking a few ag courses. I really enjoyed them . . . and a friend of my family, Dr. Potts, presented to me the idea of ag journalism. I've really enjoyed it, but am a bit concerned that my lack of ag experience will keep me from jobs in the field."

The influence of grandparents is apparent in the background of another senior major: "Both grandparents are from Godley and both have farms and/or ranches, raising commercial cattle and grain. I showed steers in the 4-H program for 10 years, exhibiting many champions across the state."

This young woman knew she wanted to major in ag journalism from the ninth grade. She writes: "I have talents and experiences in agriculture and I also learned that I had talents in English and journalism, so I decided to combine both. I know the ag field needed good representation and good 'PR' so I decided to specialize my agricultural journalism major in public relations. My efforts have paid off because upon graduation in December, I will be working as a PR director and lobbyist in Austin for an ag organization."

In response to my question about the future of the cattle industry, the perceptions of these young people appear to be surprisingly practical and "current," as shown by the comments of one:

I see the beef industry as one in trouble. Comparing the beef industry to other ag industries, i.e., pork, sheep, fruit, it has been the least innovative. Instead of making changes before the consumer demands them, the beef industry has lagged.

The future belongs to the efficient and the progressive. I have no doubts that the cattle industry will survive, but it will be in a more stream-lined, business fashion.

I think the beef industry will improve one day. But, it's going to take a tremendous PR campaign to "reconvince" people that beef isn't so bad for them. Perhaps, when the oil situation gets better in Texas, cattle prices will go up. Also, producers need to produce what the consumer wants. The successful must keep up with the time.

Katie Dickie, a former president of the organization, writes one of the most insightful opinions:

The future of the cattle industry is in marketing. Whether ranchers conform to this destiny will color how the industry survives. The cattle business—that's what it is—and people are going to have to start treating it as such. There is room for small people—if they understand what motivates the market and industry. I have lived with those who love the land and their cattle. It is a wonderful world, both the small operation and the large one. For both, marketing will be the key.

Advertising
Judy Beaullieu, a native of San Antonio, *is* the Texas Ad Agency of San Antonio, a firm which does the advertising and sales promotions for Hudson Pines Farms, of Tarrytown, New York, owned and managed by Mrs. Peggy Rockefeller (wife of David Rockefeller). Judy, now thirty-five, is the third of eight siblings, all of whom live in San Antonio. After majoring in fine arts at Stephen F. Austin University, Judy went to work for Bill West Advertising, whose specialty was purebred beef cattle. Now Judy designs and places advertisements, catalogs, and direct mail pieces for her own customers—one of whom is Mrs. Peggy Rockefeller.

I first met Judy Beaullieu in Corpus Christi when she orchestrated the "Academy Awards Sale" for Beverly Hills Simbrah.

During this weekend-long event, guests stayed at the Hershey Hotel and were treated to preliminary events of a bay cruise and elaborate buffet dinner in the historic park along the bay. Each of these events featured some presentation of the sale animals. All of the heifers in the sale bore the names of movie stars. Among my favorites was the heifer Bridget B., which Grassburr Cattle Partners purchased for their purebred herd near Bryan.[5]

In 1987 the Texas Ad Agency was chosen to do the advertising and promotion of the Hudson Pines Third Annual Production Sale held in Tarrytown, New York, in October. Pocantico Hills, the ranch headquarters in Tarrytown, is located about an hour's drive from LaGuardia Airport. The ties with Texas are numerous and essential, at least for the Texans.

In this sale in Tarrytown about 40 percent of the cattle are purchased by Texas buyers and trucked back to Texas. Most of these Texas buyers have sold cattle to Mrs. Rockefeller in the past year. Between September, 1986, and September, 1987, Hudson Pines Farms has been represented by Mrs. Rockefeller and her herd manager at five major purebred sales. In one of these, the Georges Creek Production Sale in April, 1987, they purchased four heifers for $14,000 and placed bids on several others. When I saw Rockefeller at this sale, viewing the sale offerings and visiting with other purebred breeders, the dark-haired woman stood straight and tall with a quiet dignity. She has a reputation as being a strong, no-nonsense business woman – considerably "more fierce than her husband in business matters" (Hudson Pines staff members, October, 1987). According to Judy Beaullieu (October 24, 1987), Mrs. Rockefeller is "very strong willed," and runs Hudson Pines Farms with "determination." David Rockefeller apparently has little or nothing to do with the management of Peggy Rockefeller's cattle business. He does appear at the parties which are given in conjunction with the cattle sales, but she is the hands-on manager and owner of Hudson Pines Farms.[6]

In a letter to me, Mrs. Rockefeller describes her involvement: "I can say now that my own role in the cattle business has been that of a 'hands-on' owner. I got into the business because I was anxious to do something that would maintain farmland as farmland and, at the moment, if you take our three farms into con-

Peggy Rockefeller evaluating Texas cattle for her purebred cattle program in
New York

sideration, we are probably farming around 2,000 acres. We are
involved both in cattle breeding and agriculture" (letter, Sept. 24,
1987).

The seventy-two-year-old Mrs. Rockefeller's interest in purebred beef cattle is entirely in keeping with her interests in historic
preservation. She is also interested in genetics. She writes that
"there is nothing more interesting or vital today than the study
of genetics, and those of us who are in the cattle business are
working with genetics every day of our lives."

In 1989 the program which Mrs. Rockefeller began twelve years
earlier focused on performance and the polled gene. She owns
over one hundred head of Simmental and, according to her staff,
visits her holdings upstate two to three times a week. They describe her as "by far the most independent and spirited woman
to marry into the Rockefeller family." Her spirit, her independence, and her interest in beef cattle are reflected in her frequent
cattle buying trips to Texas, where she uses her own money in
support of the historic cattle industry.

Computer Programming

It is a wet, cold day in January, 1989. Four hundred registered Simbrah, Brahman, and Gelbray cattle are selling in the liquidation of Wentz Farming Company in Olmito, Texas. The mountain of paperwork for the sale is facilitated by the use of a computer program designed by Country Line Software (Trademark) of San Antonio, Texas. The program, called Ranch Management, generates information on performance, genetics, and breeding status for each of the four hundred sale animals, as well as herd averages. Country Line Software was developed by Heddy Butler.

I met Marsha Lamb that morning in the office of Wentz Farming. Marsha says that she and Heddy Butler were in the office the previous night until 9:00 and Heddy would be in later in the morning. Heddy, as I find out later, has been commuting back and forth from San Antonio for the past week and a half helping to prepare for the sale. Marsha and her husband raise Simbrah cattle. Marsha's husband is the ranch manager for McCullum Ranch near Victoria, Texas. Marsha keeps all the books and does all the ranch's computer work for registered Simbrah cattle on an IBM using Heddy's program. Marsha says it is a lot easier than the way books were kept in the past. I also learn later that Marsha Lamb has many talents and does more than keep the books. According to Heddy Butler, Marsha also drives the big tractors with "the best" of the men.

Heddy Butler grew up riding horses on a farm near Raymondville, Texas. Now she rides a 280 Z along Highway 37 from her home office in San Antonio to her clients in the Rio Grande Valley. You will not see Heddy's business advertised. She does not need to. Her abilities and the facilitation provided by her computer software are promotion enough among the purebred Simbrah and Simmental breeders of South and Central Texas. Word of mouth is the only advertising Heddy needs to keep her very busy. She both sells and services (brings on line and keeps up to date) the software she developed.

Heddy is one of the forces of organization and new technology making the production and marketing of purebred cattle a "smarter" operation. Heddy feels that the future holds more computerization of cattle information, because agriculture has "got to be smarter." Through her program, she says, ranchers "can see things that they would not see otherwise." For example, one of her customers was able to see that a young, and heretofore unnoticed, bull was siring calves with excellent weaning weights. Another customer was able to see that a longer gestation period for bull calves was associated with the use of a particular herd sire. Most people think of gestation period as a constant, but it could be a variable—associated with the use of particular bulls.

I first met Heddy Butler at a production sale for Wentz Farming in 1986, where she was bringing their cattle records "on line." At this sale, Jenny Wentz, co-owner of Wentz Farming, and her daughter Charmaine Wentz, topped the sale with a purebred Simmental heifer, that sold for over three thousand dollars. Wentz Farming was among Heddy's first three customers. Her customers now number more than thirty, many of whom are in direct computer linkage with their breed association. This recent facilitation has many advantages. It saves money, as the breed association offers a 10 percent discount for direct line registrations, transfers, and so forth. The direct transfer of information also saves time, which can be an important advantage in quick turnaround transactions and in the exportation of cattle, which must have registration as well as health certificates for export. Finally, the direct line transfer of information to the breed association minimizes costly mistakes, as information is not keypunched, and there is less opportunity for error.

Heddy's program emphasizes: the genetic aspect, which is particularly important to breeders of Zebu and Zebu-cross cattle; weights and performance specifications; and complete breeding records. Heddy feels that "software should be tough." The programs she designs are difficult to harm. I watch her fingers play over the keyboard, adjusting the particular record she is displaying.

Heddy began with computers when, as a chemistry major at Pan American University at age thirty, she went back to school after raising four children. A professor suggested she take a course in computers. Heddy still considers herself to be a chemist, and she worked for many years for Union Carbide after her college graduation, until the plant shut down. However, she is a chemist with an important "hobby," which helps to pay the bills. Heddy says that "computer-ise is a latent disease; it only takes exposure to find out if you have it or not." Fortunately for Heddy and for the cattle industry, Heddy has been afflicted with computer-ise. Her hobby has assisted many purebred breeders enter the twenty-first century of performance records, herd evaluation, and direct-line communication. As Heddy insists, "The main thing is, don't be afraid of doing things. The computer is tough. View it as a tool, which combines features of TV, radio, VCR, adding machine, typewriter, telephone, and a whole lot more." Moreover, as Heddy says, the importance of this tool to the cattle industry is not going to diminish.

Women in the Beef Cattle Associations: Texas Cattlewomen

The Cattlewomen's Creed

Believing that the livestock industry is of basic importance to world existence, we the American National Cattlewomen dedicate ourselves to support it with our labor and finances; to encourage its producers with our understanding and love; to do all in our power to instill in the coming generation the love of the land and of life, the humility and awe before Nature and the hope and faith in the future that is inherent in cattlemen. (Texas Cattlewomen Spring Convention 1988)

The "continuing progress and prosperity of the beef industry" is the focus of the activities of the Texas Cattlewomen. Through scholarships, legislative lobbying, meetings held in conjunction with the Texas and Southwestern Cattle Raisers Association and the Texas Cattle Feeders Association, and newsletters and educational materials, Texas Cattlewomen support the beef producer. The promotion of beef and beef by-products, such as insulin, has been the objective of the Texas Cattlewomen since the early 1970s.

The organization of Cattlewomen exists at three levels: national, state, and local. All levels provide educational scholarships and educational materials. The state and local chapters also provide beef promotional activities such as a Steak-A-Rama.

At present, Texas is divided into six regions with twenty-seven local chapters: Big Country, Calico, Caprock, Circle C, Clay County, Cow Town, Golden Spread, Happy, Haskell, Heart of Texas, Hereford, Hill Country, Live Oak, Paso del Norte, Rio Grande, Rocking Red River, South Texas, Southwest Texas, Tejas, Terra Cotta, Texican, Top O'Texas, Washington County, West of the Pecos, Wichita Falls Area, Wil-dora-do, and XIT. The Texas Panhandle contains the most chapters, with nine, while South Texas has one chapter, the Texican Cattle Women.

The industry-wide concern for the market product of beef, its use and palatability, demonstrated in the multi-million dollar "beef industry checkoff" program, is of very recent origin. In this program, begun in 1987, every producer pays a one dollar fee for each head of cattle sold. The dollar is divided, with fifty cents going to the state Beef Council and fifty cents going to the Cattleman's Beef Board for the promotion of beef as a nutritious, delicious, and healthful product. According to Linda Janca, of the Texas Beef Industry Council, research showed that "the number of Americans who believe beef fits into their lifestyles increased from 59 in January to 64 percent in June" (in Brazos Valley Cattlemen's Clinic 1988). This is interpreted as a direct result of the outreach advertising, promotion, and education supported by the beef checkoff program.

There is an organization whose primary function is and has been the promotion of beef and its products since 1952. At that time, the American National Cow Belles were chartered as an auxiliary of the American National Cattleman's Association. The Texas Cow Belles, affiliated with the Texas and Southwestern Cattle Raisers Association, received their first chapter in Amarillo in 1972. During 1986 and 1987, both state and national Cow Belles voted to change their names to Cattlewomen. Many of the local chapters have followed suit.

A Cattlewoman is defined by her interest in: the promotion and welfare of the beef industry; working with legislators, producers, and consumers; and providing accurate facts and reliable information to the consumer concerning beef. Cattlewomen realized the importance of product promotion fifteen years before the rest of the industry caught up. They are now recognized as an important producer organization by the United States Department of Agriculture.

One important member of the Texican Cattle Women, an affiliate of the Texas Cattlewomen and American National Cattlewomen, Inc., is Lynne S. Neva. I met Lynne in San Antonio during the Texas Cattlewomen's Sixteenth Annual Spring Convention held at the Hyatt Regency Hotel. Lynne is the young, energetic, and knowledgeable president of the Texican Cattle Women. It is she who introduced me to the current programs and personnel of the association. She continues the heritage of concern for the product of beef, which began with the Texas Cow Belles in 1972. Archives of the Texas Cow Belles are located in

Fort Worth at the headquarters of the Texas and Southwestern
Cattle Raisers Association.

Lynne E. Neva, President, Texican Cattle Women

"We can't let it die—because then it all dies."—Lynne Neva

Lynne, at age twenty-seven, is a tireless advocate of the Texas beef
industry and the organization promoting it. In 1988, when I met
her, she was serving as president of her local South Texas organization, which had more than ninety members, having increased
from thirty-three members in 1986. Lynne says the main goal is
to "increase community awareness about the organization and its
product—beef."

Lynne grew up on a ranch. Active in 4H and FFA, she had
show steers and earned the prestigious "Chapter Farmer" award.
She says she wanted to be a veterinarian. However, Lynne began
college at Texas A&I in Kingsville, Texas, majoring in general
business. After three years she married a rancher and moved to
Laredo. She received her degree from Laredo State University.
By 1988, at age twenty-seven, Lynne was channelling her considerable energies into the Texican chapter of the Texas Cattlewomen and raising her two children, ages four years and three
months. With her business background, Lynne is constantly looking for other opportunities to support the beef cattle producer,
feeling that ranchers "can always subsidize the cattle with other
products such as mesquite."

Women are relatively visible as members of the women's auxiliary organizations, such as the women's auxiliary of the Texas and
Southwestern Cattle Raisers Association (TSCRA), which is
among the most powerful beef cattle associations in the state and
the country. For years the TSCRA has been supported by a separate women's auxiliary, which has emphasized the importance of
nutrition information and consumer education about beef.[7] The
larger TSCRA has relatively few female members and even fewer
female office holders. For example, in 1987 the organization had
only one woman as an honorary vice-president, one woman member of the Board of Directors, and no women field inspectors. The
TSCRA continues to address its membership as "Dear Cattlemen."[8]

There is some difference between the purebred and commercial sectors of the industry in the organizational representation of women. The purebred sector has more women association members than the commercial cattle associations. For example, the Texas Simmental and Simbrah Association and the International Zebu Breeders Association have many female members and, sometimes, women officers (usually secretary, but occasionally higher offices, including president). In my experience with the breed organizations, the regional or local chapters of a breed association are the most likely to have women officers. The more local the level of organization, the greater the visibility of women, in both membership and office holding. In the purebred associations there is also an association between female participation and age. The junior breed associations are well represented by young women both in membership and in activities.

The Juniors

An entire book could be written about the roles of women and girls in the junior beef cattle associations. First, it is important to recognize that these associations are vital to the industry. The junior organizations are show oriented: they encourage young people to compete in cattle shows. Most of the stock shows in Texas feature both junior and open divisions. The junior divisions is limited to young people under the age of eighteen. In the junior division ribbons and trophies often will be given for "showmanship" as well as prizes for the best cattle. The show-oriented activities of juniors provide a major market for purebred "show prospects." Young animals identified as show prospects can bring thousands of dollars above regular breeding stock. There is a lucrative and relatively stable market for show calves provided by juniors and the parents of juniors. The junior organizations also help socialize the young to the value and the values of agriculture. The junior associations support the beef cattle industry as a business and as a way of life.

I have attended several purebred cattle sales where the volume buyer or the high bidder of the sale would be a junior female, sometimes no more than nine or ten years of age. Junior females are just as likely as the males to win the major livestock shows in the junior and sometimes in the open division. Junior women are also very active in the breed associations and activities. They are much more likely to hold office in the junior associations than adult women are to hold office in the senior associations.

Young women are very visible in the junior beef associations, while mature women are largely invisible in the adult beef associations. Within the junior memberships, there appears little gender-based division of labor in the tasks performed, the honors won, or the offices held. The major junior beef cattle associations have just as many female as male members, and the young women are very active and highly competitive. In the adult beef associations, women are largely absent. Adult women tend to participate in the auxiliary organizations as described above, while the main organizations have relatively few female members and even fewer female office holders.[9] Junior women are well represented in the general associations such as the FFA and 4-H as well as in the purebred organizations.

Of thirty-four youngsters, aged twelve to seventeen, who participated in a three-day "Cow Camp" held at Texas A&M in August, 1988, sixteen were young women. The Cow Camp was sponsored by the International Zebu Breeders Association (IZBA) but was open to junior members of all breed associations, 4-H members, and FFA.[10] The camp was described as "an educational adventure" and included classes on cattle judging, showmanship, halter breaking, and marketing, as well as demonstrations of hoof trimming and a course on computerized performance records. During this camp I was invited to give a presentation on "Your Future in Agriculture." In exchange, I was allowed to obtain information on the occupational aspirations of the cow camp participants.

From the questionnaire (see appendix B) I learned that the young women in this camp were about as definite in their occupational ambitions as the males (approximately two-thirds of both the girls and boys designated a specific occupational choice). Moreover, their occupational choices tended to be highly realistic. For the young women, veterinary medicine and law were most frequently identified, with advertising a close third. For the young men, extension agent was the most frequent choice, with veterinary medicine second. It is interesting to note that none of the young women chose an unrealistic occupation such as extension agent, which at present has no or very few female incumbents.[11]

As an interesting note to this research, all but two of the girls said they wanted to live on a ranch in the future. Seven of the boys expressed a negative or conditional response to the prospect

Kendra Gayle and her little brother helping with roundup

of living on a ranch. Hence, it would appear that more of the young women than young men were oriented toward ranching as a life-style as well as a business.[12]

The number of youngsters who are visible in the junior organizations and activities is probably exceeded by those who work as "unpaid family workers" behind the scenes on Texas ranches. Like their mothers, daughters are likely to be unpaid family workers — often providing essential help with ranch chores from a very young age but seldom receiving recognition as workers.

Young Kendra rides with her mother, younger brother, and father, "pushing cows" up from a West Texas pasture. The family is on horseback from dawn to dusk, and, at age five, Kendra is expected to play an active part in herding or holding the cows, as well as to keep an eye on her younger brother. Only Kendra's father is paid for his work that day. When he is older, Kendra's brother will, most likely, also be paid for his work.[13] It is unlikely that Kendra or her mother will ever be paid workers on the ranch where Kendra's father is employed as ranch foreman. Kendra, like her mother, probably will continue to provide the "unpaid family labor" which makes it possible for "one man to run the ranch."

Women continue to provide much of the unpaid labor on Texas ranches. They continue to provide volunteer services to auxiliary cattle associations to educate and inform the public about beef, and they contribute innumerable hours in support of the junior associations where girls as well as boys participate in large numbers. The sex division characterizing women's participation in the adult beef cattle associations is not seen among the juniors. Does this mean that political clout will be more evenly divided between women and men in the beef cattle industry of the future? Not necessarily. It could simply be that there is a greater tolerance for a wide range of behaviors among children than among adults, who are expected to assume their "proper roles." It could also be a matter of economics. The purebred breeders want to sell show calves to as many competitors as possible — boys and girls. As the girls mature and marry, they will be expected to assume the same kinds of "supportive" roles presently occupied by their mothers. These maturing women will fade from view into the identities of their husbands and children.

A Theoretical Summary

In research on women and work there are two main theoretical perspectives that are used to explain variations in women's work both through time and cross-sectionally from group to group.[14] These are the individual and structural perspectives. The *individual perspective* looks for explanations of women's work within the characteristics of individuals. The *structural perspective* looks for explanations of women's work within the structures of organized society. These two theoretical perspectives have also been brought to bear on explanations of roles of farm women (Ross 1984). Hence, it appears particularly appropriate to include these perspectives in an effort to summarize the rather diverse findings of this chapter. These findings include (1) the expanding participation of women in the auxiliary occupations of the beef cattle industry, in particular those associated with the new information technology; (2) the high representation of young women in the junior beef cattle associations; and (3) the low representation of older women in the adult beef cattle associations, except as noted at the very local levels.

The individual perspective would lead us to search for an explanation of these conclusions using variables such as marital status, education, and career choice. Certainly, the growth of women's representation within the paid work force, which includes most of the auxiliary occupations, is congruent with increases in divorce and education. However, it is my feeling that these individual-level variables cannot alone explain women's greater representation, particularly in occupations such as sale barn manager and herd health veterinarian. True, women must choose these occupations. In some cases, such as veterinarian, they require extensive education. However, is choice enough? Less than thirty years ago a woman who chose to be a veterinarian would have had to seek education in another state. Texas A&M University is the only institution in Texas to offer the D.V.M. degree and for most of its history women were not admitted.[15] At present approximately 50 percent of the veterinary students at Texas A&M University are women, most from the state of Texas. The structure of opportunities had to exist before the choice of veterinary medicine could be made. Of course, tastes and aptitudes for veterinary medicine can be expected to vary among individuals, but it is no longer a universal assumption that only men can be veterinarians.[16] The structure of education in Texas now allows women the opportunity to become veterinarians. The behavior of women in choosing to enter occupations such as agricultural journalism and veterinary medicine requires that opportunities be available to women.

Similarly, the high visibility and activity of young women in the junior associations of the beef cattle industry can also be explained by a structural perspective. It is not so much that these youngsters are unconventional or nontraditional in their attitudes toward women's roles, but that they have greater opportunities for participation. It could be that opportunities for a young woman to show the prize-winning calf at a local stock show are greater now than they were in the past, but that is just the point. When the opportunities are there for women in the beef cattle industry, the women are there. This is true for both the auxiliary occupations and the junior associations. What then about the relatively low visibility and participation of adult women in the beef cattle associations?

First, this conclusion should be elaborated somewhat. Women are present in the beef cattle associations in auxiliary organizations. Women are also present in fairly large numbers in the local purebred associations. Where women are largely absent is in the large, politically oriented cattle associations such as the Texas and

Southwestern Cattle Raisers Association. No doubt some would say that women prefer to be in the auxiliary organizations (an individual-level response). This could be true for some or even all of the women presently affiliated with the auxiliary women's organizations. However, one cannot help speculating as to the membership outcome if the TSCRA stopped referring to its membership as "men" and changed its rules to include the present auxiliary of Texas Cattlewomen (formerly the Cow Belles) in its own membership. We must leave the outcome of this individual-structural debate undecided.

What will happen to women's roles in the beef cattle associations in the future could depend upon the needs of the TSCRA officers to attract the women ranchers who do not presently belong to their organization. In the interim, the relative isolation of women from the major organizations could leave them outside important networks of power, protection, and information. Insofar as the modern beef cattle industry is as much about politics as production, it could be more important for women to participate in the cattle associations to survive as ranchers in the twenty-first century. Political isolation could be less of an option in a future characterized by centralization and vertical integration of the industry.[17]

5

Ranching Women of the Future

ROLES IN THE 1990s AND BEYOND

This research suggests that women have been and are represented in the Texas cattle industry in large numbers. With modernization, the roles of women are diversifying and increasingly are associated with paid employment.

Certainly, women have been represented among cattle producers since the days of the frontier. Women were present on the frontier in far greater proportion than popular writing would acknowledge. In the 1850s and 1860s females comprised over 40 percent of the population, even in many of the frontier counties. During the early days of statehood populations were not large, nor were they heavily concentrated, but women were well represented, according to the census data presented in chapter 1. According to data from the Texas Family Land Heritage Program presented in chapter 2, some women were single pioneers who began ranches. Such a woman was Rachel Ann Northington Hudgins. Many more women ranched with their "menfolk." In those early days of statehood, there were not many occupations associated with the production of cattle. There were ranchers and there were "the hands." On all but the largest ranches "the hands" were likely to be unpaid family members. Hallie Stillwell provides an example of the duties of a "ranching wife" (chapter 2). Ranches, large and small, often rely upon the labor of all family members and also of assorted neighbors and friends during the times for "working cows," meaning times of intensive labor when cows are rounded up to be wormed, vaccinated, branded, castrated, dehorned, palpated, or bled for brucellosis testing. This is still true today. The unpaid labor of family members is highly visible. One has only to look for it.

Today the roles associated with cattle production are more diverse. To begin with, the productive segments of the industry, as distinguished from the feedlots and slaughter houses, can be differentiated as commercial and purebred.[1] Within the commercial sector there are several kinds of operations: feeder, stocker, and cow-calf. The cow-calf operation is by far the most prevalent, and it is here that most women ranchers are located. There are women ranchers represented in the commercial and in the purebred sectors of the industry. Although no purebred operators are featured in chapter 3, many interesting women can be found in this sector. One of them, Peggy Rockefeller, comes to Texas to buy seedstock for her farm located in New York. Mrs. Rockefeller also employs the advertising services of Judy Beaullieu, of San Antonio, to promote her herd of purebred Simmental cattle.

The production of cattle in the purebred sector has, since the 1960s, involved more in terms of use and analysis of information, herd health, marketing and promotion, than traditional commercial operations have. Today in the modernizing commercial sector of the industry there is also a growing emphasis on the use of performance data, certified brucellosis-free herds, telemarketing, and even the show ring as a marketing tool. All of these developments have increased the roles women play in the industry.

The occupational roles of women today are myriad and diverse. Within the cattle industry, there is a tremendous expansion of occupations in conjunction with advances in technology; there are also forces affecting the occupation of ranching. Phrased another way, there are changes in the opportunity structure of the cattle industry which have import for women's roles.

The Process of Modernization

The changes affecting the beef cattle industry are part of the process of economic development affecting the entire society. The changes have direct implications for the occupational opportunities for women.

One of these changes is increased mechanization of cattle feeding and health practices, which allows some women to ranch large operations with minimal or no assistance. All of the women ranchers profiled in chapter 3 care for their cows with little assistance. Many of the women ranchers have also made excellent use of the new information and reproductive technologies. They are using or learning to use computer-based information systems. They are also making use of palpation to cull cows with low fertility in order to increase their calf crops. In some cases these women are leaders of the industry in their application of new management techniques and in their emphasis on the production of a "lean beef" animal. Women are also disproportionately represented in the "high tech" occupations associated with advertising and promotion, reproductive physiology, and computerized information systems.

To summarize, the increased representation of women in the Texas beef cattle industry is observed in two ways. The first is increased representation of women in new occupations within the industry associated with computer technology, reproductive technology, and communications technology. These occupations include new positions associated with computer technology in the registration and evaluation of cattle, using computer-generated records such as EPDs and EBVs; new positions associated with reproductive technology in the production of superior seedstock, including artificial insemination (AI) and embryo transfer (ET); and new positions associated with communications technology in the advertising and marketing of cattle, including satellite-based sales of purebred and commercial cattle. The second area of increased representation of women is in established occupations traditionally associated with males, such as veterinary medicine. Both of these increases represent changes in the formal, paid sector of the agricultural economy.

My findings thus suggest that opportunities for women in auxiliary occupations associated with beef cattle production are increasing and that, at the same time, increased mechanization is decreasing the importance of physical strength in cattle operations. However, not all the changes taking place in the cattle industry are positive for women's participation.

Just as there are some forces which could operate to increase women's participation as ranchers and in auxiliary occupations, there are other forces which could operate to depress their participation. One of the most important factors that could lower women's participation as cattle producers is the tendency for production units to increase in size. Change favoring large-scale capital and labor-intensive ranches operates to decrease opportunities for women ranchers. Women ranchers tend to be concentrated in the smaller cattle operations of two hundred or fewer mother cows. As these small operations are forced out of the marketplace

by the larger, more cost-efficient operations, the relative representation of women ranchers could also decrease.

However, ranching is not only about economics. There are also
the forces of heritage, of values, and of life-style, all of which could
operate to maintain the smaller, noncorporate ranches most often
associated with women. Increasing numbers of ranchers, including women ranchers and women as members of ranching families,
are taking off-farm jobs to help support and maintain their ranches.
Cost efficiency does not fully explain people's relationship to their
land, nor can economics explain why some families, including
the families of women, have maintained Texas ranches through
generations of drought, declining cattle prices, and increasing taxes
and costs.

In an absolute sense, over the next decade the economists will
probably be right. Economies of scale will tend to favor the large
corporate cattle operations, some of which will be family-owned
corporations. The smaller family-owned operations of fewer than
two hundred cows will produce an even smaller share of Texas
beef cattle. Texas will no doubt boast fewer ranches and ranchers
by the year 2000 than it did in the year 1910 or even the year
1989.

One conclusion from these considerations is that the opportunity to be a rancher is, in an absolute sense, decreasing for women
as it is for men. On the other hand, opportunities for paid work
within the auxiliary occupations are increasing with development.[2]

As in other industries, expanding use of the computer is associated with an expansion of clerical jobs for women. The beef
cattle industry is no exception to this trend. Most of the ranches,
indeed almost all of the large purebred beef cattle ranches, are
using computers to enhance performance evaluation and predict
the outcome of genetic combinations and have a secretary or office manager to run the system. The cattle associations, with computerized registrations, have several positions, as do the laboratories and studs (breeding facilities where semen is collected and
stored). The modernizing cattle industry is creating more clerical
positions.[3] The new technology also introduces a self-employed
sector. Some women are creating software programs for herd management, selling the programs they have developed, and consult-
ing with the large ranches to help get their programs "on line."

Another area of expanding employment, both wage and self-
employed, is agricultural communications: advertising and jour-

nalism. The purebred breed associations publish magazines, newsletters, and promotional materials at both the national and state levels. In addition to the purebred, or special-interest publications, there are the broader trade journals and newspapers, including many I used in my research to identify women in the industry. All of these journals and newspapers employ reporters called "field representatives"—who are usually male and who sell advertising space and serve as the "ring men" in the purebred cattle auctions —and copy writers, editors, and office staff, who are usually female.

The proliferating publications thrive on and strive for increased advertising. Increasingly, the cattle business is a promotion as well as a production effort. Women's presence is strong in the areas associated with the sales and promotion of beef cattle. With the necessity for promotion of one's product has come the growth of the advertising companies. They also produce the sale catalogs that both attract and inform potential cattle buyers. Few purebred sales in this modern industry take place without a sales catalog with descriptions of every animal—pedigree, performance, and profit potential. The interest and changing enrollment in agricultural journalism on the college campus reflects the expanding opportunities for women in this field.

Chapter 4 described the expansion of jobs associated with a modernizing industry. It also described some jobs that are now open to women because of attitudinal rather than technological change. The nature of the industry is changing and so, too, are attitudes regarding what some women can do. It might be that the beef cattle industry is less constrained by the urban stereotypes of what women can and should do and, therefore, is more progressive in the jobs which are now open to women. Whatever the reason, women can be found in almost every job associated with the production of beef cattle, including cattle fitter, sales barn owner and manager, and herd health veterinarian. And as more women move into or become visible in the roles associated with knowledge and power in the industry, we can expect that attitudes will change in support of the existing structure. The only occupations in which I did not find a woman were those of cattle auctioneer (there are women horse auctioneers), beef extension specialist, and vocational agriculture teacher, although I have heard of one woman ag teacher. In the auctions women serve primarily as unpaid family labor to "clerk" and help manage

the sales. No woman is, at present, accepted with the gavel.[4] Women
are also not well represented in the powerful political structures
of the beef cattle associations either as members or as officers,
although girls are well represented in the junior associations in
both these capacities.

In some respects, the women in chapter 4 are pioneers in the
same sense as the women in chapter 2. Their frontier is different,
but they are no less courageous as they set out to conquer the
challenges of little-charted occupational territories. The same personal characteristics are descriptive of these pioneers as of the
women of the past. They are leading the way into occupations
associated with the beef cattle industry of the twenty-first century.

Changes Affecting the Industry

Major technological changes are affecting the nature of the beef
cattle industry. There are also continuous changes in environmental and economic conditions that affect the beef business.
These changes have tremendous import for the occupation of
rancher and the auxiliary occupations associated with cattle production. Some of the changes appear to be very favorable toward
an increase in women's roles. As we have seen in preceding chapters, the technological advances actually favor women's participation both as ranchers and in auxiliary occupations. The economic
climate of high beef prices would also appear to favor the increased
participation of women by making cow-calf operations profitable.
However, all of the technical and economic changes taking place
in the industry must be interpreted through an existing social structure of attitudes and beliefs about women's productive roles. This
social structure is quite conservative and must temper predictions
of an increase in the visibility of women or an expansion in their
productive roles. Major changes in the beef cattle industry taking place now must be interpreted within the existing confines
of our social structure in attempting to draw implications for the
future of women's roles.

Technological Changes
Among the most important technological changes affecting the
beef cattle industry and women's roles are changes involving herd
health and reproductive technology, changes involving computer-

generated information systems, including performance data, and changes involving video marketing and sales.

According to Carl Rugg, director of Granada Sire Services, whom I interviewed, performance information systems are the most significant change in the industry in terms of importance for the future. He feels that performance evaluation, particularly of herd sires, is and will continue to be among the most important tools for the improvement of beef cattle, both for the individual cattle raiser who can use performance data to select a herd sire and to evaluate calves within her own herd, and for the improvement of breeds. Computer-generated performance data, called "expected progeny differences" or EPDs, can also be used to "produce uniform steers that will bring premiums and replacement heifers with production efficiency" (*The Cattleman*, May 1988, 51–60).

Most breed associations provide EPD information to their members, and the rest will soon do so. Indeed, many purebred breeders have used computer-generated "expected progeny differences" for several years to select both bulls and heifers with the greatest productive potential for their herds. Expected progeny differences do not tell everything about an animal, such as its disposition or color or adaptability to environmental conditions, but they do provide "a pedigree search that goes back into the animal's background and shows the predictability for their potential to increase weaning weights, yearling weights, and milk" (*The Cattleman*, May, 1988, 52). Genetic predictions for growth, maternal, reproductive, and carcass traits are now available through most purebred breed associations. EPDs allow cattle buyers and breeders to compare animals across herds. With packers announcing that future cattle purchases will depend on carcass merit, commercial cattle raisers are now selecting bulls on carcass EPDs as well as growth EPDs.

EPDs are a sophisticated statistical tool for the selection and evaluation of beef cattle on the basis of their computer-evaluated performance as breeders and meat producers.

And, as with most computer based information technology, the tool requires technical staff to produce, disseminate, and manipulate information. The cattle breed's technical support staff are most likely to be women. For example, the American Simmental Association has a staff of twenty-six at its national headquarters in Bozeman, Montana. Nineteen of the staff positions are filled by women, and of these nineteen, ten involve record keeping (*The Register*, March, 1988, 79). The American Simmental Association also has a program of cow awards — elite, superior, and excellent — awarded on the basis of within-herd performance data (MPPAs) of 105 or greater based on a number of consecutive calves: six calves for an elite award, four calves for a superior award, and two calves for an excellent award.

Herd health is another area characterized by rapid technical advance. The computer has assisted with some of the advancement in herd health procedures brought about by the epidemic of brucellosis. Brucellosis is a sexually transmitted disease among cattle that causes cows to abort: "Brucellosis leads to spontaneous abortion, inferior calves, infertility, sterility, and decreased milk production, and it can contaminate milk, resulting in undulant fever in humans" (*Weekly Livestock Reporter*, May 5, 1988, 16A). Brucellosis is also a very serious threat to the Texas cattle industry because it is highly infectious. Texas has almost a third of the known brucella-infected herds in the country, a situation that has restricted the movement of Texas cattle and cost the state an estimated $14 million annually. Thus, it is not only a direct threat to Texas cattle, but it is a threat to the industry, which annually ships about two million cows and calves into other states. In 1986, 17.7 million cattle were blood-tested for the disease, and 8.8 million were vaccinated against it. The key to control is to vaccinate herds. All female calves are now required to be "calfhood vaccinates." There is also a state-approved certification program for entire herds. However, many producers have been reluctant to vaccinate, for several reasons: the testing requires good management practices and facilities, which many breeders, particularly those with fewer than fifty cows, do not have; independent operators are also reluctant to get involved in the "red tape" of a government-controlled program; and the current vaccine, which uses a live but less infectious form of the bacteria than field strains, can show up on blood tests, giving vaccinated cattle a false-positive result, requiring that the entire herd be quarantined (Marilyn Brown, *Weekly Livestock Rancher*, May 5, 1988). Moreover, much of the expense must be borne by the rancher, in part to pay for veterinary services.

According to Dr. Shelton (conversation of December 4, 1987), retired dean of the Texas A&M University College of Veterinary Medicine, the trends toward specialization both within disciplines and within species will mean an increase in veterinarians who specialize in bovine practice. At present, this specialization accounts for three to four percent of all practitioners. Given the importance of the brucella threat to the Texas cattle industry and economy, the demand for "large animal practitioners" and those specializing in economic animal medicine and research could be expected to increase. According to Dean Shelton, there is an "active interest on the part of young women" in the area of economic animal medicine. Women, as previously stated, presently comprise 50 percent of the student population in veterinary medicine at Texas A&M.

Given the demand for veterinarians specializing in economic animal medicine and the supply of women moving into the profession of veterinary medicine, one could predict that women will be well represented among the herd health veterinarians of the year 2000. However, there remain structural and attitudinal variables that render the supply-demand equation more complex. I do predict that the future will see an increase in the numbers of women who are represented among the economic or large animal practitioners. Many of these women will be generalists rather than specialists, meaning they will combine practices of both small and large animals. They will survive, marginally, by working very hard and very long hours in the service of clients who have both small and large animal needs—women will be disproportionately found among the generalists, the family practitioners of the year 2000. The fast track within the more elite specialties and the political clout within the professional organizations will continue to favor males. As in the practice of law and human medicine, women will increase their representation within the profession and within the professional schools. However, this representation will not be uniform among all specialties or in all ranks. Women will be concentrated in the less lucrative specialties and in general practice.

The subject of reproductive technology includes artificial insemination and embryo transplant. These technologies combine physiological advances with advances in information technology. In other words, technologies could not exist without new knowledge in reproductive physiology and new ways of handling information. According to Carl Rugg, director of a prominent bull stud during the late 1980s, a semen bank is like any other bank—it relies upon accurate information of deposits, withdrawals, and transfers (interview of May 22, 1988). Unlike a financial bank, however, it also involves the production of the "currency." That production is highly technical and, with the exception of personnel who actually participate in the physical care of bulls and the extraction of semen, the technicians employed by the large "bull studs" are women. At Granada Sire Services, six out of eleven employees are women. Three of the six are defined as technicians, including Becky Everette, the "laboratory coordinator." Three of the positions are defined as clerical and involve primarily data management and accounting.

At Medina Valley Laboratories in Castroville, Texas, women are involved in many of the same technical and clerical occupations as at Granada Sire Services. This laboratory is also involved in the technology of embryo transfer and offers both AI and palpation schools on a regular basis. At Medina Valley the embryo transfer coordinator is a woman, as are most of the technicians who process, maintain, and ship the frozen semen.

Women are also represented at the AI schools. Approximately 12 percent of the graduates of the AI schools are women. Sarah Buxkemper, owner of Prescription Simbrah, was the first woman to graduate from the AI school offered by the American Breeders Service (ABS) in 1959 (conversation of June 6, 1987). She was also the second woman to graduate in animal science from Oklahoma State University (formerly Oklahoma A&M), in 1955 (at that time Texas A&M did not admit women students). Although women are not likely to be employed as AI technicians upon graduation, they are frequently the "unpaid" AI technicians and reproductive specialists on their own farms and ranches.

The use of video is of growing importance in the marketing of commercial and purebred cattle. Videotapes have been used by some of the larger purebred breeders for two to three years to promote their operations and sell selected prize cows and bulls (I acquired my first video on a purebred Brahman ranch in 1986). Most brokers and cattle "consultants" also practice selective employment of video tapes and believe the results can be positive. Gary Cross, a purebred cattle broker, considers video tapes to be an important tool of the marketing trade and predicts that the technology "will be more and more a part of the sales business" (conversation May 21, 1988). Carl Rugg suggests that video could be particularly important in the development of international markets (conversation of May 23, 1988).

Video technology has been brought to the sales arena in yet another way. Auctions using video tapes and broadcast over commercial satellites to receiver dishes are becoming fairly frequent in the sale of commercial cattle and occasionally in the purebred sector (one recent sale of Beefmaster cattle was broadcast from Las Vegas via satellite). These "satellite sales" have a number of advantages in geographically expanding markets, bringing the sale to more potential buyers, and reducing the stress on cattle. Cattle can now be viewed and sold in the pasture instead of transported to and concentrated in sale barns. The old method of sale-barn selling is geographically fixed in a particular community, requiring not only the transportation and concentration of large numbers of cattle with the attendant stress, but also that the cows be "run through the ring." This process can also be a source of stress for the cows and for the people responsible for getting the cows into and out of the sales ring. The new method of satellite sales will render some jobs obsolete, particularly those associated with the physical handling of cattle through the sales rings. However, it will create other positions associated with the processing of information and with cattle marketing. Many of these jobs will be data-management in function and clerical in pay, and many will be filled by women.

According to the *Gulf Coast Cattleman* (June, 1988, 9), the responsibility for leaner beef will be pushed back from the retailer to the packer and the cattle producer. All three levels will be concerned for the consumer demand for lean meat. As we have seen, the market share for beef has been decreasing, with only a slight reversal of this trend associated with the recent promotional efforts of the cattle producer associations, for example, the NCA and the TSWCA, and the Beef Checkoff Program administered by the BIC. The market demand is for a leaner product. Moreover, the lean must come from the beef animal itself, bred for reduced internal fat or marbling, as well as from the reduction of external fat or "trim." This is a challenge to the beef cattle producer: to produce an animal that will "weigh out" with lean muscle rather than with fat. Retailers do not want to lose money by having to trim large amounts of external fat from the carcasses they buy from packers. Packers do not want to lose money by "hot trimming" large amounts of external fat from the animals they kill. So, it is predicted that live animal buyers, such as Excel Corporation, will pay a premium for heavily muscled lean beef animals, containing no more than 25 percent Zebu genetics.

Moreover, genetics will largely determine the amount of internal fat or marbling that will be produced per unit of feed. Some purebred and commercial producers have been concerned for the production of lean beef animals for several years. Ahead of their time in recognition of what the industry needs, these producers have frequently been women. Disproportionately, women have been at the forefront of producers concerned for the production of lean beef. Purebred producers such as Sarah Buxkemper, of Prescription Simbrah, have long used carcass data in the selection and evaluation of herd sires. Another purebred Simbrah breeder, Judith Turlington, has received statewide recognition for the production of high-performance herd sires at the Houston Livestock Show All Breed Bull Sale. In 1987, T25, a twenty-month-old bull calf sired by Judith's herd sire, Bones, was judged by a group of twenty cattlemen as the best "ear" (Brahman-influenced) bull and was ranked sixth out of all 115 bulls in the sale (*Farm and Ranch*, March 6, 1987, 24). The genetic production of lean beef animals and the use of the modern tools of reproduction, including AI and ET, and performance, including carcass EPDs, will continue to be a top priority for the industry. According to the *Gulf Coast Cattleman*, "Recent consumer studies . . . are revolutionizing the way beef is grown, processed and marketed" (Feb., 1987, 24) and it is predicted that premiums will soon be paid for leaner animals. Recognition of and education about the importance of nutrition in the beef product has long been the concern of the Texas Cattlewomen and disproportionately of the woman rancher. Women have been the leaders in the recognition of the importance of lean beef to the Texas cattle industry.

Economic Changes
After a period of depressed cattle prices, the commercial sector of the industry is economically healthy, with prices for young calves bringing over $1.00 a pound. This compares to only $0.56 a pound in 1985. However, the purebred sector of the industry is recovering from the depression of 1985–87 more slowly. The fancy ballroom purebred cattle sales, with prices for a single animal ranging from $10,000 to $250,000, are mostly a thing of the past. The investor money is gone, and so are the tax advantages which attracted the money. The oil money, real estate money, and banking investments in syndicated cows have gone the way of the cattle drives. Indeed, the lines between the elite purebred operations and the commercial cattle ranches are fast disappearing.

Many purebred breeders have long relied on commercial ranchers to buy their purebred bulls. Now with the investment-oriented markets gone, most purebred producers are oriented toward the commercial markets to sell seedstock as well as bulls. By the late 1980s the purebred bull market was very strong as the commercial people could afford to pay unusually high prices for their herd bulls. It was not unheard of to find commercial breeders paying $2,000 for purebred bulls. Moreover, there was evidence that the purebred market for seedstock was strengthening as more pure-bred producers could afford to pay well for replacement heifers because of the strength of the purebred bull market.

Another important factor in the beef industry is the price of land. Although low land prices are not necessarily reflected in tax evaluations, by the late eighties more rangeland was available, and at relatively low prices. In Central Texas, it was possible to buy rangeland at less than $1,000 per acre. All of these economic changes looked good for the future of the cattle rancher. For the first time in a long time, rangeland was available and affordable.

Economically speaking, in 1989, for the first time in almost a decade, it was possible to make a living raising cows. It was also possible to buy or expand rangeland. Some banks were even providing substantial lines of credit to their ranching customers because of the good cattle market. Unfortunately, economics was not the only "voice" in the choir of circumstances affecting the cattle rancher in the late 1980s.

Environmental Changes
In 1988, drought and range fires were affecting many areas of the state—killing cows and forcing the sale of many others. Hay was in short supply, as the first cutting for 1988 was not possible in large areas without rain. This condition extended into 1990 for some areas of the state. Moreover, drought in the major corn- and wheat-producing states can send feed prices soaring. In June, 1988, experts were saying that farmers were suffering from the worst drought for that time of year since 1922, when record-keeping began.

These environmental conditions can and do lower the prices of feeder and stocker cattle in areas of Texas, although, in general, the commercial market remained strong heading into the 1990s. The very large operations actually are the ones that could be most injured by the cash flow dilemmas brought about by natural disaster. They have already been hard hit by losses of investor capital and tax advantages, and it might well be the smaller operations that survive the environmental crises. The large operations have no incentive to hold on – there are no longer the attractive advantages of losses to offset gains in other areas of income – and could find high prices a good reason to liquidate. In addition, the large corporate ranches often lack the marketing "flexibility" of the smaller ranches. Those which can dig in and survive the vicissitudes of weather could be the winners in a very short-supply post-drought market. Of course, the large corporate ranches would still have advantages of credit and capital not available to the smaller operators. But there are the intangibles of "taste" for ranching and commitment to a way of life, which could have a hand in the final determination of who stays and who goes.

Although some would simply see the expansion of small "suburban" ranches as another form of urban blight, suburbanization of ranching could be a significant trend of the future. Demographers have already noted the first reversal in this century of the migration trend from rural to urban areas. In some part, the movement from urban to rural areas probably reflects the growth of "part-time ranchers," whose ability to raise cows is made possible by an urban job. These part-time ranchers have two environmental constraints: they must be close enough to an urban area to be employed, and they must have enough acreage to support cattle (without a year-round feeding program). Both these needs are satisfied by the suburbanization trend.

The cattle market is a most volatile and speculative marketplace. Climatic conditions are always precarious; they can worsen or improve dramatically over a given year. Even in a drought year one good rain can bring on some of the grasses for autumn forage. Hence, in the final, sociological, analysis, it could be that noneconomic and nonclimatic conditions will decide the composition and characteristics of tomorrow's ranchers. Attitudinal and other "social" factors of upbringing and opportunity may, in the final analysis, be the most important variables in the equation predicting the future of the occupation of ranching.

Attitudinal Changes

Angela Bonifazi gave an important insight into ranching: "Ranching is not just a job; it is a way of life." Today, ranching is no less esteemed – to the contrary, ranching as a way of life may be more highly regarded than ever before. To own cows is to enter a world of hallowed tradition. This is particularly true in Texas, where the "cowboy" represents independence and self-sufficiency, and now, in recent years, glamour. To be associated with the raising of beef cattle is more prestigious today than ever in the highly romanticized past of the industry. This "glamorizing" of the industry may represent part of its attraction to men and also to women. However, more than the "urban cowboy" syndrome, I believe ranching represents the basic values of a culture that, while predominantly urban in its present, is rural in its roots and traditions.

Ranching is basically a family endeavor. It represents and reinforces the importance of the family unit. Most activities of ranching are family-oriented. This includes everything from the working of cows to the social parties and sales. Ranching is a family tradition and a tradition of families. Many of the women in the industry are part of this tradition.

The attitudes of women themselves must be taken into account in any predictions of their future roles in the industry. Certainly, the young women I have met in my research demonstrate an enthusiasm and respect for ranching. I do not think this will change. However, the positive attitudes toward ranching as an occupation and as a way of life do not mean the women I talked with consider it possible for themselves. Very few young women see ranching as a viable or available occupation. This includes those who have been active in the junior breed associations. Their abilities and experience with cattle do not appear to inform an expectation that they will be able to make a living in the industry, or willing to give up the traditional expectations of marriage, home, and children, which, realistically, will involve a more urban orientation and life-style because of the concentration of jobs, schools, hospitals, and so forth in urban areas. The attitude of the young women is that ranching may be desirable as a way of life, but it is not practical as an occupation either for themselves or their husbands. This attitude is reflected in the opinions about the future of the mature women I interviewed. For the most part, they do not feel that their ranches will survive them. This is true either because of the changing environmental conditions, such as urbanization, or because of the aspirations of the young themselves for more prestigious and lucrative urban-based occupations such as law and medicine.

Ranching is a precarious occupation and is increasingly rare as a sole avenue of income. My finding of a fairly negative orientation toward ranching as an occupation coexisting with a very positive orientation toward ranching as a way of life is similar to the attitude found among farming and ranching women in the USDA-NORC survey reported in chapter 1. In this survey, the majority of women reported high satisfaction with farming or ranching as a way of life and low satisfaction with farming or ranching as a way to make a living.

Implications for Women's Roles

What do all the changes in the technical-economic-environmental sphere, and lack of change in the attitudinal sphere, mean for women's roles in the next century? In the area of technology, increased mechanization would appear to be a positive condition for women's presence on cattle ranches. Women who ranch alone or with spouses and children often use mechanization to advantage. In direct contradiction to theories of economic development, I predict that mechanization will increase rather than depress women's participation as cattle raisers. The other aspects of technological development discussed here, including the widespread use of artificial insemination, performance records, and telemarketing will also act to increase women's presence as ranchers and in the auxiliary occupations. Similarly, the economic condition of high prices with few "investor incentives" will act to support women's participation. I also predict that women — who represent predominantly small, noncorporate operators — will survive the present environmental crises as they have survived them in the past. Women will continue to own and operate Texas farms and ranches because of demographic and individual influences. Women will inherit the land as daughters and as surviving spouses. Families with few children are more likely to have daughters as inheritors. And women still tend to outlive men by almost ten years, in all ethnic groups. Both of these conditions favor the role of women as owners of Texas farms and ranches.

I predict that, similar to the past, approximately 25 percent of Texas farms and ranches will be owned solely by women in the year 2000. Of this 25 percent, about one-half of the women will both own and operate their ranches, meaning that they will perform all or most of the tasks and all of the decisions for their operations. Of course, the wealthy will have the option of hiring ranch managers to perform the more arduous labor. Even on these ranches, women owners usually have, and will continue to have, an active role in the management decisions, if not the day-to-day tasks of their operations.

Although I predict that the percentage of ranchers who are women will remain fairly consistent with the past, this percentage will be based on a decreasing number of cases. The number of Texas farms and ranches is decreasing. In June, 1987, the Texas Agricultural Statistics Service reported 160,000 farms and ranches. This figure represents a 10 percent decline since 1985 and the lowest figure reported since records began in 1910 (*Weekly Livestock Reporter*, September 10, 1987, 10). Women will continue to be represented among the ranchers of Texas; they could even increase their representation slightly, but in the year 2000 there will be very few full-time ranchers. Most of the noncorporate full-time ranchers of the year 2000 will be retired from other occupations. Some, relatively few, will be young and independently wealthy, most from sources other than cattle.

In the year 2000 the occupation of rancher will be predominantly a part-time occupation for those below the age of fifty-five who are not independently wealthy. Demographics, including the low fertility rate, the small size of families, and the greater longevity of women, will favor women among the older full-time ranchers. Most of the "new breed" of part-time ranchers under age fifty-five will be men. This is true because men are most likely to be employed in occupations that provide both the discretionary income and time to support ranching interests.

There are several depressants to women's participation in the new occupation of part-time rancher. Two of these are economic: the structural trend toward large ranches, and the concentration of women in low-paid occupations. Women are less likely to be awarded the credit necessary to operate a large commercial cow-calf endeavor. Nor are women represented in the lucrative specialties of law and medicine to the same extent as men. The specialties of corporate law and medical surgery supply a disproportionate number of modern "ranchers" to the purebred sector of the industry. A third depressant is social: sex-role expectations.

Among the major depressants to women's participation as ranchers while they are "young," under age fifty-five, is the continuing social constraint of sex-role expectations. Although very young women, or girls under the age of twenty, are highly visible in the junior livestock organizations associated with production agriculture, their presence does not continue into the adult organizations. Women continue to be largely invisible in the adult commercial and purebred cattle associations. This is particularly true in the commercial sector of the industry. Moreover, most women, even those presently ranching, appear to accept the traditional sex-role expectation for women. In some cases, these ranching women simply see themselves as "different." In some cases, they feel they have had no choice. Few of the young people seem prepared for the price of "being different." They expect to marry, and realistically, they expect that marriage will mean an urban rather than rural life-style. What the future holds for these young people on an individual level, I cannot say. However, they will, in some future day, be more likely than their urban-reared contemporaries to return to the land. They, more than others, are likely to choose professions compatible with some future ranching activity, including veterinary medicine, agricultural journalism, animal science. These young women are also significantly more likely than their contemporaries to make up the 12 percent of "sole operators" of the future who are women.

Young women with ranching backgrounds are more likely to enter the auxiliary occupations serving the cattle industry than they are to become ranchers. They are more likely to major in agricultural journalism, animal science, or veterinary medicine. They are more likely than those with urban backgrounds to seek jobs that have to do with agriculture. Many of these jobs, located in urban areas, are, as we have seen, clerical in nature. Being located in the "pink ghetto," the clerical positions are unlikely to provide the kind of rewards required to purchase land or cattle even with the encouragement and support of spouses. I am not optimistic about the future for the young women who have and are today accomplishing so much in the FFA, 4-H, and junior breed associations.

Except for those who inherit the actual resources for ranching— land, cattle, equipment—the thousands of young cattle breeders in 4-H, FFA, and the junior breed associations will leave their ranching experience behind as they take up the responsibilities of providing for a family. Their productive roles in agriculture will be preempted by their productive roles as workers in the non-agricultural sectors of the economy and by their roles as mothers and wives. A few will take the place of ranching parents. Some will return to the land as cattle producers, or the "wives of ranchers" when they retire. Most will not, in the future, be associated with production agriculture. They will, for a while, have shared a rich heritage—a heritage of self-sufficiency and strength, which they will need in their future as workers, as mothers, and as wives in the pioneer world of the twenty-first century.

Conclusions

High prices and good agricultural economy are positive factors influencing the occupation of rancher. However, it is doubtful that any but the very large "corporate type" ranches and the independently wealthy "ranching families" will survive in the occupation of truly independent rancher. Most ranchers of the future will combine cattle raising with careers as business owners or lawyers or physicians or, occasionally, professors. Ranchers will be those whose other occupations allow them the pleasure of ranching, not as a hobby (for hobbyists as defined by the IRS will not survive) but as a way of life supported by other income(s). Some of the surviving ranchers will be women. They will be strong women with a strong sense of heritage. They will be women who are independent in spirit and independent in wealth.

Women will continue to provide essential services, including managerial decisions as well as physical labor, on family-owned farms and ranches. I expect that these family-owned operations, employing the labor of all family members, will continue to be the majority of Texas beef cattle operations, although their production share probably will lessen. In other words, these family-owned ranches will produce a smaller share of the total beef cattle.

The large, corporate-type ranches will, most likely, continue to be the most cost-effective production units of the future, and they will, like corporate America, be male dominated. However, the incentives for the corporation are unidimensionally economic —they will not stay "when the going gets tough." The incentives for the family ranch are multidimensional: life-style, values, community. Families and individuals with a love of heritage will stay in the business of ranching when the corporations with lessening profit margins and fewer tax incentives will not. Except for those corporations which are both product-diverse (for example, Granada Corporation) and vertically integrated (producing beef for their own food markets, such as McDonald's Corporation), the production of beef cattle is not, under present economic conditions, particularly attractive to corporations. Of course, this could change with expanded trade agreements, for example, between the United States and Japan. However, for the next few decades, I predict the predominance of the family-owned and family-managed operations as the backbone of the Texas beef cattle industry. I also predict that women will continue to own and manage many of these ranches.

Women will be co-owners of almost 60 percent of Texas ranches in the year 2000 — the family-owned ranches of the future. Women will be the sole owners of approximately 25 percent of the ranches of the future. Of these, women will both own and manage about one-half or 10 to 12 percent of the ranches of the future. These ranches will be concentrated among the small and medium-sized cow-calf operations of fifty to two hundred mother cows. The other 20 percent of Texas farms and ranches will be owned solely by men, including most of the large, vertically integrated corporate ranches of the year 2000.[5] Although one can expect that there will be a few women represented among the very large family-owned cattle operations in the future, there is no reason to believe that women will be represented among the executive personnel of the nonfamily corporations in any way which is markedly different from the way they are represented (or not represented) in other industries of corporate America.

The growth sector of the beef cattle industry is in the auxiliary occupations, particularly in those occupations associated with the growth of computer-based information systems, reproductive technology, and advertising. These occupations are predominantly held by the self-employed, owners of advertising businesses, cattle fitting businesses, and sales management businesses. Some of these occupations are professional, such as herd-health veterinarian. However, many of the new occupations are in the "pink collar" ghetto of clerical work.

These new clerical positions will provide little economic independence or economic security for the workers who occupy them. Thirty-five percent of all employed women in the United States are already clustered in clerical positions, many working long hours at important work for low pay. Insofar as clerical positions associated with the beef cattle industry are similar to other clerical jobs, they will be characterized by low pay and little chance of advancement into managerial positions. Managerial positions will continue to be occupied by men, who will continue to depend on the knowledge and expertise of the women working for them in the Texas cattle industry, as in the larger society.

Some notable women are visible in what can be considered male-dominated occupations associated with the industry such as economic animal medicine, cattle fitter, sale barn manager. However, most of these women are self-employed. One conclusion is that women in male-dominated sectors of the industry have to own their own businesses in order to be in them. These women are not likely to be employed in administrative positions by others. And their numbers are certainly not large. Kanter's theory of work organizations tells us that unless the numbers of women increase significantly in male-dominated areas, the few "token women" will not likely survive the situationally induced stress of being tokens (Kanter 1977). But even if these women can survive the barriers perceived by Kanter for token women in male-dominated occupations, one cannot presume that these few women will or can perpetuate long-term changes in opportunities for women.

There remain relatively few women sales managers, cattle fitters, and herd health veterinarians. There are still relatively lucrative and powerful occupations within the industry that have few women at present. These include cattle auctioneer (there are horse auctioneers who are women) and agricultural extension beef cattle specialist (the women agricultural extension personnel are mostly home economists).

This research does not conclude on a tide of unbridled optimism. The evidence is mixed, suggesting an expanding of job opportunities for women in the industry, but not necessarily an increase of opportunities in the most desirable and lucrative jobs. Women could still be playing predominantly supportive roles in the beef cattle industry of the year 2000 and beyond.

Occupations associated with the beef cattle industry will tend to conform to and be informed by the structures and attitudes of the larger urban-oriented society. This is a society in which women do not share equally in the recognition and rewards of work, although women supply labor both to the formal sector of the paid economy and to the informal, all but invisible, economy of unpaid family labor and "volunteer work."

The women ranchers I have met in the course of my research on the Texas cattle industry have been self-sufficient and independent. They take pride in the work they do and in the heritage they represent. However, even these women do not know the extent to which women have contributed to this important and historic industry. Even they do not know the extent to which the industry of the future will be supported by the contributions of women.

Women will provide and process the information for the industry of the year 2000. They will help generate and implement the health and reproductive technology for a safe and nutritious beef product. Women will promote and implement the sales of cattle through advertising, video, and telemarketing. Women will show cattle in the purebred shows and support sons and daughters in the FFA and 4-H and junior breed associations. Women will play vital roles in the beef cattle industry of the year 2000 as they have made major contributions to the past. However, their contributions will not ensure recognition.

It remains to be seen how the roles of women will be rewarded by the beef cattle industry of the future. Certainly, we have a long way to go in providing adequate recognition for women's roles in the past and in the present. I would like to think that this book will provide a beginning toward the recognition of their roles in the future. When you look for women on the Texas range you will find them . . . working there.

Appendixes

Appendix A. Tables

Table 1. Women's Involvement in Farm Tasks (percent by row)

Task	Percent Responding Task is Done: Regularly	Occasionally	Never	N[a]
Plowing	11	26	63	2,257
Fertilizing	5	12	83	2,377
Other fieldwork	17	25	58	2,281
Harvesting crops	22	29	49	2,351
Care of animals	37	29	34	1,944
Running farm errands	47	38	15	2,483
Purchasing farm supplies	14	23	63	2,455
Marketing farm products	15	18	67	2,380
Keeping farm records	61	17	22	2,489
Household tasks	97	2	1	2,499
Supervising farm work of family members	24	26	50	2,060
Supervising farm work of hired hands	11	25	64	1,643
Raising home garden or animals	74	14	12	2,350
Care of children	74	13	13	1,846

[a]Total excludes those who say task was "not done." Taken from Jones and Rosenfeld (1981, Table 2.4)

Table 2. Women's Involvement in Farm Decisions (percent by row)

| Final Decisions | Who Decides | | | |
	Respondent	Husband	Both	Nᵃ
Buy or sell land	3	39	58	2,166
Rent land	2	48	50	1,915
Buy major equipment	2	52	46	2,426
Produce something new	3	58	39	2,174
When to sell products	4	60	36	2,349
New production practice	3	62	35	2,125
Take off-farm job	41	7	52	1,959

ᵃTotal excludes those who say decision was "not made." Taken from Jones and Rosenfeld (1981, Table 2.7) *ble 3*. Sex Composition of Texas Counties of 200 or More Inhabitants: ›50–80.

County	Total Population[1]				Percent Female			
	1850	1860	1870	1880	1850	1860	1870	1880
₊nderson	2,284	10,398	9,229	17,395	48.6	46.6	49.5	48.0
₊ngelina	945	3,574	3,985	5,239	48.1	48.5	50.3	49.2
₊ransas				996				49.0
₊rcher				596				40.6
₊tascosa		1,471	2,915	4,217		43.4	48.1	46.0
₊ustin	2,286	6,225	15,087	14,429	43.7	45.6	48.1	48.6
₊andera		387	649	2,158		43.7	43.1	48.3
₊astrop	2,180	4,415	12,290	17,215	44.4	45.8	47.4	47.7
₊aylor				715				40.4
₊ee		831	1,082	2,298		44.0	49.2	46.4
₊ell		2,061	9,771	20,518		45.7	47.8	47.8
₊exar	5,633	13,057	16,043	30,470	39.4	46.3	49.5	47.2
₊lanco		1,183	1,187	3,583		45.6	47.3	45.6
₊osque		1,712	4,981	11,217		46.5	47.2	46.0
₊owie	1,271	2,401	4,684	10,965	43.7	44.5	49.4	46.9
₊razoria	1,329	2,027	7,527	9,774	38.1	41.3	48.0	47.4
₊razos	466	1,713	9,205	13,576	45.7	45.1	48.7	47.5
₊rown		244	544	8,414		45.5	47.1	46.8
₊urleson	1,213	3,680	8,072	9,243	45.4	45.6	47.2	47.0
₊urnet		2,252	3,688	6,855		43.7	46.8	47.2
₊aldwell	1,654	2,870	6,572	11,757	26.2	46.3	48.7	48.0
₊alhoun	857	2,228	3,443	1,739	45.9	43.5	48.9	50.0
₊allahan				3,453				41.3
₊ameron	8,469	5,955	10,999	14,959	40.8	44.0	45.7	47.4
₊amp				5,931				48.4
₊ass	3,089	4,936		1,674	44.5	45.9		48.2
₊hambers		995	1,503	2,187		46.5	48.8	46.0
₊herokee	5,389	8,849	11,079	16,723	45.6	47.7	49.9	49.5
₊lay				5,045				45.2
₊oleman			347	3,603			37.5	43.7
₊ollin	1,816	8,217	14,013	25,983	46.1	46.7	48.3	45.7
₊olorado	1,534	4,326	8,326	16,673	44.3	44.6	48.9	49.2
₊omal	1,662	3,837	5,283	5,546	44.3	46.0	47.2	48.4
₊omanche		648	1,001	8,608		46.0	47.6	47.0
₊oncho				800				37.0
₊ooke	219	3,391	5,315	20,391	47.0	46.9	47.4	46.6
₊oryell		2,360	4,124	10,924		46.0	49.6	48.0
₊allas	2,536	7,591	13,314	33,488	46.5	45.5	48.2	46.0
₊awson		821				34.2		
₊elta				5,597				47.1

County	Total Population[1]				Percent Female			
	1850	1860	1870	1880	1850	1860	1870	188
Davis			8,875				48.3	
Denton	631	4,780	7,251	18,143	47.4	47.2	47.8	46
De Witt	1,148	3,465	6,443	10,082	44.6	45.5	48.6	49
Dimmit				665				41
Duval			1,083	5,732			42.3	44
Eastland				4,855				44
Edwards				266				41
Ellis	902	4,142	7,514	21,294	47.1	45.3	46.5	46
*El Paso		4,022	3,671	3,845		40.6	44.8	49
Encinal			427	1,902			39.1	41
Erath		2,307	1,801	11,796		47.0	47.8	47
Falls		1,896	9,851	16,240		44.6	48.0	47
Fannin	3,260	7,496	13,207	25,501	45.3	46.5	48.0	46
Fayette	2,740	7,808	16,863	27,996	45.0	45.8	48.5	48
Fort Bend	974	2,007	7,114	9,380	42.1	43.0	49.9	47
Franklin				5,280				48
Freestone		3,268	8,139	14,921		46.5	49.0	48
Frio			309	2,130			46.9	43
Galveston	3,785	6,707	15,290	24,121	47.2	44.0	48.7	49
Gillespie	1,235	2,703	3,566	5,228	41.3	45.4	47.5	47
Goliad	435	2,541	3,628	5,832	36.6	45.4	50.6	48
Gonzales	891	4,891	8,951	14,840	45.0	43.6	48.6	48
Grayson	1,822	6,892	14,387	38,108	45.9	45.8	48.0	47
Gregg				8,530				48
Grimes	2,326	4,838	13,218	18,603	45.2	43.7	47.4	49
Guadalupe	1,171	3,689	7,282	12,202	44.5	47.7	48.2	47
Hamilton		463	733	6,365		47.1	46.7	47
Hardin		1,162	1,460	1,870		44.4	49.3	49
Harris	3,756	7,008	17,375	27,985	45.4	43.3	49.6	49
Harrison	5,604	6,217	13,241	25,177	45.7	46.8	49.3	49
Hayes	259	1,329	4,088	7,555	42.9	45.2	48.0	46
Hidalgo		1,157	2,387	4,347		43.2	45.0	47
Hill		3,003	7,453	16,554		45.8	48.1	46
Hood			2,585	6,125			47.3	47
Hopkins	2,469	6,755	12,651	15,461	47.1	47.9	49.4	47
Houston	2,036	5,239	8,147	16,702	46.9	46.4	50.2	48
Hunt	1,477	6,053	10,291	17,230	47.0	46.7	48.7	46
*Jack		950	694	6,626		44.5	46.1	46
Jackson	627	1,396	2,278	2,723	43.2	43.0	48.9	48
Jasper	1,226	2,426	4,218	5,779	46.1	45.8	51.3	49
Jefferson	1,504	1,684	1,906	3,489	45.4	41.7	49.8	47
Johnson		3,792	4,923	17,911		46.5	47.7	46
*Jones				546				41
Karnes		1,844	1,705	3,270		42.6	43.8	46

County	Total Population[1]				Percent Female			
	1850	1860	1870	1880	1850	1860	1870	1880
Kaufman	982	3,403	6,895	15,448	46.5	47.0	48.5	47.0
Kendall			1,536	2,763			46.8	46.0
Kerr		585	1,042	2,168		41.0	42.6	47.2
Kimble				1,343				45.1
Kinney			1,204	4,487			34.9	37.6
Lamar	2,893	7,294	15,790	27,193	47.6	47.0	49.2	48.0
Lampasas		874	1,344	5,421		44.4	46.1	47.6
La Salle				789				35.7
Lavaca	1,139	4,238	9,168	13,641	45.6	44.8	49.0	48.9
Lee				8,937				48.2
Leon	1,325	4,161	6,523	12,817	44.9	45.4	48.0	47.7
Liberty	1,623	2,102	4,414	4,999	45.5	45.0	49.8	47.7
Limestone	1,990	3,464	8,591	16,246	44.3	46.3	47.4	48.0
Live Oak		508	852	1,994		42.1	41.7	47.0
Llano		1,047	1,379	4,962		46.4	46.7	46.9
McCulloch				1,533				43.3
McLennan		3,802	13,500	26,934		43.8	49.0	48.0
McMullen			230	701			40.4	35.8
Madison		1,563	4,061	5,395		47.4	48.8	48.7
Marion		1,960	8,562	10,983		43.4	48.0	49.1
Mason		606	678	2,655		40.8	47.8	44.9
Matagorda	913	1,347	3,377	3,940	45.3	43.9	48.3	47.8
Maverick		704	1,951	2,967		38.4	43.0	43.2
Medina	881	1,732	2,078	4,492	34.2	46.4	48.0	46.7
Menard			667	1,239			20.1	34.7
Milam	2,469	3,632	8,984	18,659	42.2	46.2	47.5	47.7
Montague		814	890	11,257		47.9	45.3	46.0
Montgomery	1,439	2,668	6,483	10,154	45.4	45.9	48.5	48.3
Morris				5,032				47.8
Nacogdoches	3,758	5,930	9,614	11,590	45.8	45.5	50.0	48.6
Navarro	1,943	4,105	8,879	21,702	42.8	45.6	47.9	46.8
Newton	1,255	2,106	2,187	4,359	47.2	48.0	49.7	49.0
Nolan				640				42.0
Nueces	650	2,689	3,975	7,673	33.8	43.4	45.9	53.6
Oldham				287				38.0
Orange		1,495	1,255	2,938		41.9	51.1	45.2
Palo Pinto		1,394		5,885		46.2		43.4
Panola	2,676	5,417	10,119	12,219	46.6	46.5	49.2	49.0
Parker		3,991	4,186	15,870		46.5	48.5	45.3
Pecos				1,807				41.1
Polk	1,542	4,098	8,707	7,189	45.3	46.8	50.6	49.8
Presidio		574	1,636	2,873		24.0	30.2	38.7
Rains				3,035				47.7
Red River	2,493	5,491	10,658	17,194	48.2	46.7	49.5	47.9

County	Total Population[1]				Percent Female			
	1850	1860	1870	1880	1850	1860	1870	188
Refugio	269	1,360	2,324	1,585	46.8	43.9	45.8	47
Robertson	670	2,739	9,990	22,383	45.4	45.6	47.2	47
Rockwall				2,984				45
*Runnels				980				38
Rusk	6,012	9,670	16,916	18,986	44.2	46.2	49.3	49
Sabine	1,556	1,600	3,256	4,161	49.0	47.4	50.4	49
San Augustine	2,087	2,377	4,196	5,084	45.1	47.2	50.1	48
San Jacinto				6,186				49
San Patricio		525	602	1,010		43.8	43.7	47
*San Saba		824	1,425	5,324		48.2	48.4	48
*Shackelford			455	2,037			49.4	41
Shelby	3,278	3,885	5,732	9,523	46.9	46.9	48.7	48
Smith	3,575	8,408	16,532	21,863	45.7	47.0	49.8	49
Somervell				2,649				47
Starr		2,396	4,154	8,304		42.4	41.2	44
*Stephens			330	4,725			42.4	45
Tarrant	599	5,170	5,788	24,671	40.7	46.4	48.0	46
*Taylor				1,736				43
*Throckmorton				711				41
Titus	3,168	7,209	11,339	5,959	48.1	46.0	48.7	48
*Tom Green				3,615				35
Travis	2,336	4,931	13,153	27,028	44.0	45.8	44.6	47
Trinity		3,432	4,141	4,915		46.9	50.1	49
Tyler	1,476	3,377	5,010	5,825	46.9	47.0	49.0	49
Upshur	2,712	6,851	12,039	10,266	46.9	45.8	50.1	48
Uvalde		479	851	2,541		39.5	44.1	43
Van Zandt	1,308	3,453	6,494	12,619	47.6	48.0	49.3	47
Victoria	1,396	2,757	4,860	6,289	43.7	46.0	50.3	50
Walker	2,663	4,056	9,776	12,024	45.7	43.2	47.9	44
Waller				9,024				48
Washington	3,166	7,271	23,104	27,565	45.2	45.1	48.3	49
Webb		1,397	2,615	5,273		45.4	42.8	42
Wharton	510	646	3,426	4,549	42.5	42.9	49.8	49
*Wheeler				512				25
*Wichita				433				31
Williamson	1,410	3,638	6,368	15,155	46.0	46.3	48.2	46
Wilson			2,556	7,118			46.4	46
Wise		3,031	1,450	16,601		47.2	46.9	46
Wood		3,963	6,894	11,212		47.1	50.0	47
*Young		500	135	4,726		46.0		46
Zapata		1,248	1,488	3,636		46.7	45.8	45
Zavala				410				48

[1] The figures for 1850 and 1860 are for whites only.
*Indicates counties which might be considered "frontier."

Table 4. Registrants of the Texas Land Heritage Program
(percent by row)

Year	Women Sole Owners Percent	(N)	Women Part Owners Percent	(N)	Male Sole Owners Percent	(N)
1983*	29.2	(49)	50.6	(85)	20.2	(34)
1982	21.4	(22)	41.7	(43)	36.9	(38)
1981*	31.1	(19)	44.3	(27)	24.6	(15)
1980	17.5	(17)	53.6	(52)	28.9	(28)
1979	22.4	(11)	49.0	(24)	28.6	(14)
1978–1977	20.3	(27)	48.1	(64)	31.6	(42)
1976	22.1	(34)	46.7	(72)	31.2	(48)
1975*	25.6	(98)	52.4	(200)	22.0	(84)
1974	23.9	(132)	30.0	(166)	46.1	(255)
Total						
Percent	24 percent		43 percent		33 percent	
(N)	(409)		(733)		(558)	

from Elizabeth Maret, *Texas Cowgirls,* 1986

Table 5. Women's Involvement in Ranch Tasks (percent by row)

Task	Percent Responding Regularly	Occasionally	Never	(N)[a]
Plowing	5.2	25.6	66.7	(39)
Fertilizing	8.2	16.3	75.5	(49)
Other fieldwork (no machinery)	8.2	18.4	71.4	(49)
Harvesting crops	13.4	31.2	53.3	(45)
Care of animals	36.5	33.0	30.6	(52)
Supervising farm work family members	24.4	26.7	46.7	(45)
hired farm labor	23.1	18.0	59.0	(39)
Growing garden or animals for family consumption	56.8	20.4	20.4	(44)
Running farm errands	47.3	36.4	14.5	(55)
Purchasing farm supplies	22.6	18.9	58.5	(53)
Marketing farm products	24.1	18.5	57.4	(54)
Keeping farm records	70.9	16.4	21.8	(55)
Working on family or in home business	37.5	12.5	45.8	(24)

[a]Total excludes those who say task was "not done" on their operation.

Table 6. Women's Involvement in Ranch Decisions (percent by row)

| Final Decisions | Who Decides | | | |
	Respondent	Husband	Both	(N)[a]
When to sell products	4.1	47.0	48.9	53
New production practices	– –	51.1	48.9	51
Buy and sell land	4.7	29.3	66.0	48
Rent land	3.5	25.1	71.3	43
Major farm equipment	1.5	51.7	46.8	50
New crop or breed	2.2	53.9	43.9	49
Take off-farm job	44.5	9.1	46.4	39

[a]Total excludes those who say decision is not made on their operation.

Appendix B. Data Collection

Interview Guide

INTERVIEW OF:
  (when)

NAME OF RANCH   BRAND

LOCATION
  distance

  major geological formations

SIZE AND TYPE
  land in acres

  type and number of cattle

  gross annual proceeds

BACKGROUND
  original size

  original cost

  when acquired by family

  when acquired by respondent

OPERATION
  type of participation (own, manage, etc.)

  how long sole, supervisory, partnership

  degree of participation
    in such TASKS as planting, plowing, harvesting, applying fer-
    tilizer, supervising hands, taking care of stock, marketing, pur-
    chasing, bookkeeping, care of household

    in such DECISIONS as buying and selling stock and/or land
    and/or other ranch products, whether to buy equipment, feed
    and/or try a new production practice

Husband's participation (incl. off-ranch employment)

Respondent's off-ranch activities (incl. employment, volunteer)

membership and offices in ranch related Associations

number and tasks of hired hands

EDUCATION
formal: where
       when (for how long)
informal (most impt. ranch-related)

MARITAL AND FAMILY
Maiden name

Husband(s) name(s)
  when married
  how long married

CHILDREN (grandchildren)
number

age

interest in ranching

REASONS FOR RANCHING

FUTURE OF RANCHING INDUSTRY (in general and in own case)

MOST IMPORTANT CHARACTERISTIC(S) OF A RANCHER
(anything special for/about women ranchers?)

MAJOR OBSTACLES TO (OR) SUPPORTS FOR SUCCESS

HOBBIES

PHILOSOPHY

MISC.

IZBA Cow Camp Participants   August 3–6, 1988

NAME: _____
              first   last

AGE: _____   ADDRESS: _____
                                    _____
                                    _____

What cattle related organizations do you belong to? (e.g., FFA, 4-H, IZBA Jrs.) _____

Do your parents own or manage cattle? (yes or no) _____

Do you want to go to college? (yes or no) _____

   For those who say yes, where do you want to go? _____

   For those who say yes, what do you want to study? _____

What job or occupation do you want after you finish school?

_____
_____
_____

Do you think this job or occupation will allow you to own cattle? (Why or why not?)

_____
_____
_____

Do you think you will want to get married and have a family? (yes or no) _____

   For those who say yes, how many children would you like to have? _____

Do you want to live on a ranch? (yes or no) _____

Notes

Introduction.

1. In research terminology this discovery of something new in the process of inquiry is termed "serendipity." It is one of the most exciting aspects of research and often among the most fruitful.

2. There are humorous stories connected to every research project. Some of mine involve trying to get photographs of the women as they worked. One such experience involved a sale of Longhorn cattle. The sale manager and owner of the ranch where the sale was held was Mrs. Betty Lamb. Some of the cattle sold that day had horn spans of four feet or more, and some of them did not like the narrow chute which led into the sale ring. When a Longhorn gets upset there are horns everywhere! When one particularly obstreperous cow tried to climb up and over the chute leading into the ring, most of the visitors and hands tried to get away from the area. Mrs. Lamb, however, rushed over to the chute to get the cow back in and, of course, I followed with camera set to try to get an "action photograph." There was a lot of action all right: someone got in between my camera and Mrs. Lamb, and the action photograph showed one heck of a set of horns and a tall gentleman exiting the area. Mrs. Lamb did indeed persuade the cow to get back in the chute, but the best photograph of that day only shows her a safe distance from the cattle on the sale podium. See the photograph of Mrs. Lamb and her Longhorn bull in Chapter 4.

3. Some of the letters I received from friends and relatives of Texas ranchwomen in response to my announcements are themselves valuable sources of information.

4. The volatility of the cattle industry during the period between 1986 and 1989 proved to be a continuing challenge to the efforts of observation, as many cattle breeders experienced drastic changes in fortune during that time.

Chapter 1.

1. Prior to the Civil War, cattle were usually driven into Louisiana, which was a less profitable venture (Pool 1975).

2. This number had declined to 127,000 in 1989 (*Southern Livestock*, 1 (26), Jan. 26, 1990, p. 1).

3. *1984 Texas Livestock, Dairy and Poultry Statistics*, Texas Department of Agriculture, June, 1985, p. 21.

4. Under the practices of intensive or rotational grazing, stocking rates can be considerably higher.

5. An operation is defined as "any place having one or more cattle on hand during the year" (USDA 1985, 6).

6. These data are for 1984 as published by the U.S. Department of Agriculture Bulletin 228, published in June 1985.

7. Feedlots with capacities of one thousand head or more accounted for 98 percent of the cattle fed in Texas in 1985 (1988–89 Texas Almanac 1987, 583). Large amounts of capital are required for feedlot operations, and the "economics" of this sector of the cattle industry have led to fewer and bigger operations. Most of these are concentrated on the High Plains because of the supplies of sorghum and other feeds. Slaughter houses also tend to be concentrated geographically and economically and tend to be located, not too surprisingly, near feedlots. Whenever cattle have to be hauled or transported, they tend to "shrink" or lose considerable weight. There is also about a 2 percent death loss associated with long distance travel by truck.

8. Fl cows are a first cross between genetic pools of the bos indicus and bos tarus. Because they are a first-generation cross, they maximize heterosity.

9. The reasons for this are open to debate. A colleague, Dr. Ruth Schaffer, suggests that the "element of risk" makes ranching a particularly romantic enterprise. This is particularly true for city dwellers. The ownership of land, privacy, and relations to animals, particularly to horses, can explain the appeal of ranching to people whose lives are defined in cities.

10. Even my computerized spell check program identified "cattle-woman" as incorrectly spelled and recommended that I replace cattle-woman with "cattleman."

11. In community property states like Texas, property inherited from parents and other relatives is considered to be "separate property."

12. On this issue, see Maret and Copp (1982).

13. Very few agricultural enterprises in the United States practice subsistence farming, i.e., grow what they need for food. Most agricultural operations produce products for cash, and they tend to be specialized in relatively few products. There is, therefore, no reason to expect farm families to spend less for items like food and clothing than nonfarm families. Indeed, there are many costs, such as medical care and insurance, which are likely to be higher for resident farm families than for urban dwellers.

14. I found the term "go-fer" to be in fairly common use among ranching women. It refers to the tremendous amount of time spent "going for" various objects (e.g., tools, trimmers, medicines, feed supplies, etc.) and services.

15. Findings for farm and ranch women are consistent with other research on variability in the division of labor based on sex (see, for example, Maret 1985).

Chapter 2.

1. Studies of women's labor on the farm in the late 1970s and early 1980s included the possibility of diverse roles. For example, Boulding (1979) classified three role types: the farm wife, the woman farmer, and the farm housewife. Lodwick and Fassinger (1979) presented a six-fold classification of Michigan farm women, while Buttel and Gillespie (1984) identified eight types of roles among New York farm families.

2. The image of women as "homemakers" and "secondary workers" remains even given the rapid increase in female-headed families – families in which there is no adult male to occupy the provider role.

3. This perception is not only external to agricultural people, but reflected by them. For example, although the majority of farm and ranch women report that they could operate their farms and ranches alone, very few of them report their occupations as farmers. Most report their occupations as "wife-mother-homemaker."

4. In the preface to a popular account of a pioneer ranching woman, the writer refers to this woman as "the daughter" of a rancher, "the sister" of a rancher, "the wife" of a rancher, and "the mother" of a rancher. She is not referred to as a rancher in her own right.

5. I would also like to recommend the writings of Evelyn King (1983) on "Women on the Cattle Trail and in the Roundup." I have found that in the modern roundups of family-owned Texas ranches, most or all of the family members participate, including the very young and the very old, as well as whatever neighbors can be "rounded up."

6. The following materials were taken from personal interviews with Hallie Stillwell in October, 1984, and from the *Big Bend Country* by Virginia Madison (1955), to which Hallie contributed.

7. Note that even these figures underrepresent the presence of women because many women, particularly black women, were not counted. For an excellent treatment of the representation and contributions of black women as well as nonblack women, see Luchetti and Olwell's *Women of the West* (1982).

8. On April 21, 1836, the concluding battle for Texas Independence, the Battle of San Jacinto, was fought on the ranch of Peggy McCormick.

Chapter 3.

1. Three of these cases were "no response" because the ranch land was leased rather than owned.

2. Unfortunately, many tasks characteristic of ranching, such as fence building and animal husbandry tasks, are not differentiated in this survey of farm and ranch women. For example, we do not know the extent to which women participate in "working cows" when cows are rounded up to be branded, vaccinated, castrated, and dehorned.

3. As seen in Chapter 4, sometimes the "inheritance" is reversed as children who become active in the junior associations bring their parents into or back into the cattle business. Often in my observations, it is mothers who provide initial support for their children's FFA or 4-H projects. Sometimes as a result of growing interest after children become involved, women become cattle breeders themselves. Usually these women have agricultural backgrounds, although not necessarily in beef cattle.

4. There are no black women identified in the subsample of women on beef-cattle ranches in the USDA-NORC survey (N=213). There are 6 American Indians and 7 Hispanic women in the national subsample (N=213). In the regional subsample of ranching women (N=55), 2.5 percent are Hispanic.

5. The shortage of other sources of labor on family-owned ranches might help to explain this encouragement.

6. Of the other women I interviewed, about 60 percent were unmarried. Thus, increasing the number of women in the chapter would not have changed the distribution by marital status.

Chapter 4.

1. Texas Department of Agriculture, 1984, 49.

2. I once bought a semen interest in a bull, Tex-Mex, that was valued at $68,000. After this bull won reserve grand champion at the Simbrah Celebration in Austin, Texas, another semen interest was auctioned off. At this same sale, part interest in one of Granada's bulls, Headliner, sold to a Houston bank for $250,000.

3. The last time I saw Robin Sibley she was working at Academy Surplus in College Station. She was getting ready to take a job with a race horse training outfit, having been unable to find steady work as a cattle fitter or ranch hand. I do not think she finished her degree at A&M.

4. One of the functions of the Cow Belles, recently renamed the Texas Cattlewomen, is to support education.

5. Grassburr Cattle Partners is the registered name of my purebred cattle company. The "partners" include husband, Sam, and son, David. As with most cattle operations this one is also a family business.

6. Hudson Pines Farms has been a political force in keeping the Texas markets open and accessible. In 1986 efforts by the Rockefellers kept New York from shutting its borders to Texas cattle because of blue tongue. Mrs. Peggy Rockefeller plays an important role in maintaining the cattle connection between Texas and New York.

7. I visited the headquarters and archives of the Texas and Southwestern Cattle Raiser's Association in Fort Worth in the spring of 1986 to investigate the status and roles of women depicted in their publication, the *Cattleman*, and in their organization minutes and convention records. The TSCRA has an annual convention and trade show in the spring. The Cow Belles also meet at that time, although their meeting is separate.

8. In all the correspondence I received from this organization, I was always addressed as "dear cattleman," although the name of the organization stipulates the sex-neutral term of "cattle raisers." There are many subtle messages women get about the legitimacy of their participation. This one says men. Several of the commercial women ranchers told me this male identity is one reason they do not belong to the association. They feel the organization will not do much to help women members.

9. Only one in four of the Southwestern ranch women interviewed in the USDA-NORC survey was a member of a farm or ranch organization.

10. See "IZBA to host '88 Cow Camp," in *Farm and Ranch*, July 29, 1988, page 8.

11. As of March, 1990, there are three women extension agents in the state.

12. Of the fifty-five Southwestern ranch women interviewed in the USDA-NORC survey, 84 percent said they were "very satisfied" with ranching as a way of life. However, only 45 percent said they were very satisfied with ranching as a way to make a living.

13. In my research comparing the OCG data from the Blau and Duncan study on American men to NLS data on American women (Maret 1988), I found that a much higher proportion of resident farm males than females reported their first occupation to be farm labor. This was true even though a similar proportion of females and males reported farm origins. The solution to the puzzle was that resident farm men were more likely to perceive and report their work on the farm as a first job. While it is likely that females performed similar tasks, it appears that these tasks were unpaid and not perceived of as a job.

14. Sometimes, in demographic explanations for variations in women's labor force participation through time, it is more common to hear the terms supply and demand. However, supply is basically an individual set of circumstances pertaining to the worker's characteristics, while demand is basically a structural set of circumstances which are

characteristic of organizations and beyond the control of individuals.

15. Sonja Oliphant Lee, who now resides in Lubbock, Texas, is said to be the first woman to have entered the veterinary school as a student in 1963.

16. Before women were allowed the opportunity to be veterinarians, it was not possible to disprove the assumption that only men had the abilities and desires to be veterinarians.

17. On this issue, see Jimmy Guillot, "Contract Poultry Growers Offer Warning to Cattlemen." *Gulf Coast Cattleman* 56 (March, 1990): 10–11.

Chapter 5.

1. Many of the larger operations combine a purebred and a commercial segment.

2. At the risk of sounding overly theoretical, one could hypothesize that opportunities to own the means of production will decrease for women in the beef cattle industry, while the opportunities to be a wage and salary worker will increase.

3. This information would appear to support the "optimistic view" that new technology will lead to the creation of clerical jobs (on this issue, see Hodson and Sullivan 1990, 323). It also supports the view that these clerical jobs will be predominantly female or "feminized" (Hodson and Sullivan 1990 311–16).

4. Since writing this conclusion, I have indeed come across information about a woman auctioneer who sells cattle at the livestock auction in Huntsville, Texas. I have not followed up on this lead, but it could again reflect an important principle of my research. When one looks for women, they can usually be found! A corollary of this might be that researchers must look for women if the women's contributions are likely to be recognized.

5. If the Japanese continue to buy Texas ranches as they have begun to do (for example, with Granada), I would revise this figure upward.

References

Government Documents and Technical Reports

Albrecht, Don, and Howard Ladewig. 1982. *Texas Agriculture: A Statewide Overview of Its Importance, Diversity, and Changing Structure*. Departmental Technical Report No. 82–2. College Station: Department of Rural Sociology and Texas Agricultural Experiment Station.

Jones, Calvin, and Rachel A. Rosenfeld. 1981. *American Farm Women: Findings from a National Survey*. Report no. 130. Chicago: National Opinion Research Center.

Salant, Priscilla. 1983. *Farm Women: Contribution to Farm and Family*. Agricultural Economics Research Report no. 140. Economic Development Division, Economic Research Service, U.S. Department of Agriculture, in Cooperation with Mississippi Agricultural and Forestry Experiment Station, Department of Agricultural Economics, Mississippi State University.

Texas Department of Agriculture. 1976. *Family Land Heritage Directory, 1976*. Austin, Texas.

Texas Department of Agriculture. 1978–83. *Family Land Heritage Honorees*. [annual volumes]. Austin, Texas.

Texas Department of Agriculture, Family Land Heritage Program. 1974–83. *Texas Family Land Heritage Registry*. Vols. 1–9. Austin, Texas.

Texas Department of Agriculture and U.S. Department of Agriculture. 1985. *1984 Texas Livestock, Dairy and Poultry Statistics*. Compiled by Texas Crop and Livestock Reporting Service. Austin, Texas.

Texas Department of Agriculture and U.S. Department of Agriculture. 1986. *1985 Texas County Statistics*. Bulletin 240 (October). Austin: Agricultural Statistics Service.

U.S. Bureau of the Census. 1978. *1978 Census of Agriculture*. Washington, D.C.: U.S. Government Printing Office.

U.S. Department of Agriculture and National Opinion Research Center. 1972. *American Farm Women Survey.* Washington, D.C.: U.S. Government Printing Office.

Personal Communications, Interviews, and Observations

Agricultural Communicators of Tomorrow. Texas A&M University. Interviews, November, 1986.

American Breeders Service A. I. Management School. Brenham, Texas. Observation, August, 1986.

Angelina Farms First Annual Production Sale. April 4, 1987. Crockett, Texas. Observation of Dorie Yates, co-owner and graduate of TCU Ranch Management Program.

Beaullieu, Judy. Texas Ad Agency. Interview, October 24, 1987. San Antonio, Texas.

Bonifazi, Christine. Letter, May 8, 1984. Interviews, June and October, 1984. Ranch.

Box "O" Farm, Hall "O" Fame Sale. April 30, 1988. Caldwell, Texas. Observation of Mrs. LaVera Sanders, owner.

Britten Auction Seminar. Bryan, Texas. Observation, June, 1987.

Butler, Heddy. Observation at Wentz Farming Fall Fiesta, September 4, 1987. Observations and interview at Wentz Cattle Dispersal, Olmito, Texas, January 16 and 17, 1989.

Butler, O. D. Texas A&M University. Interview, January, 1986.

Buxkemper, Sarah. Grassburr Cattle Partners. Interview, June, 1987.

Cattleman's Beefmaster Sale, Bryan Livestock Commission. February 2, 1986. Observation of Marla Hendricks, D.V.M., sale veterinarian.

Crain, Lexie. Letter, March 23, 1988: history of the Cow Belle Organization.

Everette, Becky. Granada Sire Services. Observation, June, 1987.

Godbolt, Maurine. Interview, October, 1984. Ranch.

Hendricks, Marla, D.V.M. Grassburr Cattle Partners. Observations and interviews, June–July, 1987.

IZBA Cow Camp. Observations and interviews, August, 1988. Texas A&M University.

Lamb, Betty, owner and sale manager. Observation, May 30, 1987.

1st Annual Lamb Ranch Texas Longhorn Production Sale. Ranch, Somerville, Texas.

LaRue Douglas Cattle Fitting School. Georgetown, Texas. Observation, July, 1986.

Lawhorn, Martha Ann Clement. Interview, August, 1984. Ranch.

Luedecke, Mary Ann. Letter, November 18, 1984.

Nava, Lynne S. Letter, March 29, 1988.

Neville, Angela. Grassburr Cattle Partners. Interview, December, 1985.

Rockefeller, Peggy. Letter, September 4, 1987.

Rugg, Carl. Granada Sire Services and Grassburr Cattle Partners. Interview, May, 1988.

Stillwell, Hallie. Interview, October, 1984.

Turlington, sale consignor. "Christmas Package" Sale, Hotel Sofitel, Houston. Observation, December 7, 1985.

Uptmore, Adele. Sale Barn, West, Texas. Observation and interview, July, 1986.

Warnke Walls, Cindy. Observations and telephone interview, September–November, 1985.

Williams, Ethel. Letters, August 17, October 8, 1984. Interview, November, 1984. Ranch.

Worthington, Jackie. Interview, September, 1986. Ranch.

Corporate Newsletters and Publications

American Red Brangus Journal. *1985 Membership Directory.* March, 1985.

―――. *1986 Membership Directory.* March, 1986.

―――. *1988 Membership Directory.* March, 1988.

Angelina Farms First Annual Production Sale (program). Crockett, Texas. April 4, 1987.

Angus. 1986. *50th Anniversary Texas Angus Association Directory.*

Box "O" Farm, Hall "O" Fame Sale (program). Caldwell, Texas. April 30, 1988.

Butler, Heddy, Country Line Software. News Letter #1. September 3, 1986.

Cattleman's Beefmaster Sale (program). Bryan Livestock Commission, Bryan, Texas. February 2, 1986.

"Christmas Package" Sale (program). Hotel Sofitel, Houston. December 7, 1985.

Donnell Ag Genetics. 1988 Beef Sires. Catalog.

1st Annual Lamb Ranch Texas Longhorn Production Sale (program). May 30, 1987.

Flat Top Ranch Guaranteed Complete Dispersion (program). Walnut Springs, Texas. June 22, 23, and 27, 1987.

Granada Genetics (brochure). Texas Division. Marquez, Texas.

Granada Invitational (program). Wheelock, Texas. June 13, 1987.

Granada News (Granada Corporation). Spring, 1987.

Guera Bros. Simbrah and Zebu Legacy of Champions Sale (program). Linn, Texas. November 8, 1986.

Hudgins, J. D., Inc. (brochure). Hungerford, Texas.

International Stockmen's School 22nd Annual Program. Houston, Texas. February 18–21, 1988.

International Zebu Breeders Association Membership List as of July 1985 (mimeograph).

Medina Valley Genetics Newsletter. January, 1988.

New Breed Industries. *1988 Sire Directory.*

Pride Cattle Company (program). December 12, 1987.

Producers Newsletter (Producers Cooperative Association, Bryan, Texas). December, 1987.

Satellite Cattle Exchange. Video Auction of Stocker and Feeder Cattle. Televised from Amarillo, Texas, on Telstar 303. February 25, 1988.

Satellite Cattle Exchange Newsletter. Vol. 1., no. 1. February 26, 1988.

SideSaddle (National Cowgirl Hall of Fame and Western Heritage Center, Hereford, Texas). 1979, 1986.

Simbrah Celebration '85 (program). Austin, Texas. November 8–9, 1985.

Texas and Southwestern Cattle Raisers Association. 111th Annual Convention and Trade Show (program). San Antonio, Texas. March 13–16, 1988.

Texas Brahman Association. *Texas Brahman Association Directory 1988.* Margaret Watkins, secretary-treasurer.

Texas Cattlewomen. Sixteenth Annual Spring Convention (program). San Antonio, Texas. March 13–14, 1988.

Texas Limousin Association. *1984–1985 Texas Limousin Directory.* Crowley, Texas.

Texas Longhorn Breeder Association of America. *1985 Directory.* Fort Worth.

Texas Simmental Association. *Texas Simmental Association 15th Anniversary Edition. 1984–1985 Directory.* San Antonio.

Texas Simmental/Simbrah Association. *1985 Directory.*

Texas Simmental/Simbrah Association Newsletter. November, 1987. February, June–July, 1988.

Texican Cattle Women 1988. (Directory). An Affiliate of Texas Cattlewomen and American National Cattlewomen, Inc.

Texican Statement (newsletter). February, 1988. March, 1988.

Wentz Farming Company Partnership Liquidation Sale (program). Olmito, Texas. January 16–17, 1989.

Wentz Farming Fall Fiesta (program). Olmito, Texas. September 4, 1987.

Periodicals

Abilene Reporter-News. Feb. 9, 1986.

American Beef Cattleman. October, December, 1987. March, 1988.

American Red Brangus. June, December, 1987. June, 1988.

American West. August, 1987.

American Zebu Journal. June–July, October–November, 1987. Winter, 1987–88.

Bryan–College Station Eagle. 1985–88.

Cattleman, The. 1986–88.

Cattle Today. February 20, 1988.

Dallas Morning News. March 17, 1985.

Farm & Ranch. 1985–88.

Farm and Ranch Messenger. October, 1987. March, 1988.

Farm Journal. June–July, 1983. September, 1988.

Forbes. August 30, 1982.

Gulf Coast Cattleman. 1987–88.

Hereford Brand. June 24, 1986.

Houston Chronicle. January 27, 1985.

Insite. July, 1986.

Livestock Network Reporter. February, 1988.

National Geographic. August, 1985.

Progressive Farmer. 1987–88.

Register, The. 1987–88.

RoundUp. October, December, 1987.

Showbox, The. April, 1986.

Simbrah World. 1987–88.

Simmental South. 1988.
Texas Agriculture. 1988.
Texas Farmer Stockman. 1987–88.
Texas Hereford. March, 1988.
Texas Monthly. February, 1985. November, 1987.
Ultra. July, 1985.
U.S. News & World Report. March 21, 1988.
Weekly Livestock Reporter. 1986–88.

Meetings, Speeches, and Presentations

Brazos Valley Cattleman's Clinic and Trade Show. *Proceedings.* April 29, 1988. Texas Agricultural Extension Service.
Maret, Elizabeth. "Changing Trends for Women in Agriculture: Involvement and Invisibility." Paper invited for Second International Ranchers Roundup. San Angelo, Texas. August, 1983.
Maret, Elizabeth. "Texas Cowgirls." Paper presented at Liberal Arts Forum, Texas A&M University, College Station. April, 1986.
"Trail Boss, The." Proccedings of "Ranching through the Eyes of Texas." 1988 Annual Meeting of the Society for Range Management, Corpus Christi, February 21–26, 1988.
White, Larry D., and A. LeRoy Hoermann, ed. Proceedings of 1982 International Ranchers Roundup, Del Rio, Texas. August 9–13, 1982.
Wilkening, Eugene, and Nancy Ahrens. "Involvement of Wives in Farm Tasks as Related to Characteristics of the Farm, the Family, and Work off the Farm." Paper presented at Annual Meetings, Rural Sociological Society. August, 1979.

Books and Articles

Akerman, Joe A., Jr. 1982. *American Brahman: A History of the American Brahman.* Houston: American Brahman Breeders Association.
American Breeders Service. 1983, 1986. *A. I. Management Manual.* Second ed. DeForest, Wis.: Division of W. R. Grace & Company.
Applebaum, Herbert, ed. 1984. *Work in Market and Industrial Societies.* Albany: State University of New York Press.

Beers, Howard. 1937. "A Portrait of the Farm Family in Central New York State." *American Sociological Review* 2:591–600.

Blood, Robert. 1958. "The Division of Labor in City and Farm Families." *Journal of Marriage and the Family* 20:170–74.

Boserup, Ester. 1970. *Woman's Role in Economic Development*. New York: St. Martin's Press.

Boulding, Elise. 1980. "The Labor of U.S. Farm Women: A Knowledge Gap." *Sociology of Work and Occupations* 7:261–90.

Boulding, Elise. 1984. "United States Farm Women." Pp. 179–98. in *Work in Market and Industrial Societies*, ed. Herbert Applebaum. Albany: State University of New York Press.

"Brangus: The Tough Breed for the Tough Customers." 1990. Supplement to *Weekly Livestock Reporter*, January 18.

Brewer, Michael. 1981. *The Changing U.S. Farmland Scene*. Population Bulletin 35. Washington, D.C.: Population Reference Bureau.

Bunton, Mary Taylor. 1939. *A Bride on the Old Chisholm Trail in 1886*. Reprint 1985. San Antonio: Naylor Company.

Butler, Heddy. 1986. *Cattle Country Ranch Management System*. San Antonio: Country Line Software.

Carpenter, Liz. 1987. *Getting Better All the Time*. New York: Simon & Schuster.

Crawford, Ann Fears, and Crystal Ragsdale. 1982. *Women in Texas*. Burnet, Tex.: Eakin Press.

Crawford, Richard P., and Richard J. Hidalgo, eds. 1977. *Bovine Brucellosis: An International Symposium*. College Station: Texas A&M University Press.

Day, James, Billy M. Jones, Dayton Kelley, W. C. Nunn, Rupert N. Richardson, Harold B. Simpson, Martha Anne Turner, and Dorman H. Winfrey. 1972. *Women of Texas*. Waco: Texian Press.

Dobie, J. Frank. 1964. *Cow People*. Austin: University of Texas Press.

Erickson, John R. 1980. *Panhandle Cowboy*. Lincoln: University of Nebraska Press.

Exley, Jo Ella Powell. 1985. *Texas Tears and Texas Sunshine*. College Station: Texas A&M University Press.

Fears, Ann, and Crystal Sasse Ragsdale. 1982. "A Texas Cattle Queen." In *Women in Texas*. Burnet, Tex.: Eakin Press.

Flora, Cornelia B. 1985. "Women and Agriculture." *Agriculture and Human Values* 2 (Winter): 5–12.

Glenn, Norval D. 1967. "Massification versus Differentiation: Some

Trend Data from National Surveys." *Social Forces* 46 (December): 172–80.

Gulliot, Jimmy. 1990. "Contract Poultry Growers Offer Warning to Cattlemen." *Gulf Coast Cattleman* 56 (March): 10–11, 28–29.

Haney, Wava G., and Jane B. Knowles. 1987. "Women and Farming: Changing Roles, Changing Structures." *Signs: Journal of Women in Culture and Society* 12:797–800.

Hodson, Randy, and Teresa Sullivan. 1990. *The Social Organization of Work.* Belmont, Calif.: Wadsworth Publishing.

Holland, Ada Morehead. 1988. *Brush Country Woman.* College Station: Texas A&M University Press.

International Stockmen's School. 1988. *Beef Cattle Science Handbook 22.* Edited by L. S. Pope. Bryan, Tex.: International Stockmen's Educational Foundation.

Jackson, Jack. 1986. *Los Mesteños: Spanish Ranching in Texas.* College Station: Texas A&M University Press.

Jones, Calvin, and Rachel Rosenfeld. 1981. *American Farm Women: Findings from a National Survey.* Chicago: National Opinion Research Center.

Jordan, Teresa. 1984. *Cowgirls: Women of the American West.* Garden City, N.J.: Doubleday & Company.

Joyce, L. M., and S. M. Leadley. 1977. *An Assessment of Research Needs of Women in the Rural United States.* University Park: Department of Agricultural Economics and Rural Sociology, Pennsylvania State University.

Kanter, Rosabeth Moss. 1977. *Men and Women of the Corporation.* New York: Basic Books.

King, Evelyn. 1983. *Women on the Cattle Trail and in the Roundup.* Bryan, Tex.: Brazos Corral of the Westerners.

Leach, Joseph. 1952. *The Typical Texan: Biography of an American Myth.* Dallas: Southern Methodist University Press.

Luchetti, Cathy, with Carol Olwell. 1982. *Women of the West.* St. George, Utah: Antelope Island Press.

Lyson, Thomas A. "Sex Differences in Recruitment to Agricultural Occupations among Southern College Students." *Rural Sociology* 46 (Spring, 1981): 85–89.

McMurtry, Larry. 1968. *In a Narrow Grave: Essays on Texas.* New York: Simon & Schuster.

Madison, Virginia. 1955. *Big Bend Country.* Albuquerque: University of New Mexico Press.

Madison, Virginia, and Hallie Stillwell. 1968. *How Come It's Called That?* New York: October House.

Malone, Ann Patton. 1983. *Women of the Texas Frontier: A Cross-Cultural Perspective.* Monograph No. 70, Southwestern Studies. El Paso: Texas Western Press.

Maret, Elizabeth. 1983. *Women's Career Patterns.* Latham, Md.: University Press of America.

Maret, Elizabeth. 1985. "Changing Domestic Responsibilities among Married Women." Pp. 31–40 in E. Busch and J. Busch, eds., *The Family in the Information Society.* Louisville, Ky.: Systems Science Institute.

Maret, Elizabeth, and Lillian Chenoweth. 1979. "Women: The Invisible Texans." *Texas Agricultural Progress* 25 (Summer): 28–30.

Maret, Elizabeth, and James Copp. 1982. "Some Recent Findings on the Economic Contributions of Farm Women." *Rural Sociologist* 2 (March): 112–15.

Matthews, Sallie Reynolds. 1936. *Interwoven.* Reprint 1982. College Station: Texas A&M University Press.

Myres, Sandra. 1985. "Cowboys and Southern Belles." *Texas Humanist* 7:15–19.

Nixon, Jay. 1986. *Stewards of a Vision: A History of the King Ranch.* Kingsville, Tex.: Privately printed.

Pate, J'Nell L. 1988. *Livestock Legacy.* College Station: Texas A&M University Press.

Pearson, Jessica. 1980. "Women Who Farm: A Preliminary Portrait." *Sex Roles* 6:561–74.

Pool, William C. 1975. *A Historical Atlas of Texas.* Austin: Encino Press.

Roach, Joyce Gibson. 1977. *The Cowgirls.* Reprint 1990. Houston: Cordovan Corporation.

Ross, Peggy. 1985. "A Commentary on Research on American Farmwomen." *Agriculture and Human Values* 2 (Winter): 19–30.

Sachs, Carolyn E. 1983. *The Invisible Farmers.* Totowa, N.J.: Roman and Allanheld.

Sachs, Carolyn E. 1985. "Women's Work in the U.S.: Variations by Regions." *Agriculture and Human Values* 2 (Winter): 31–38.

Smith, Dorothy E. 1989. "A Peculiar Eclipsing: Women's Exclusion from Man's Culture." Pp. 3–21 in R. D. Klein and D. L. Steinberg, eds. *Radical Voices.* New York: Pergamon Press.

Smith, Erwin E., and J. Evetts Haley. 1952. *Life on the Texas Range.* Austin: University of Texas Press.

Sterber, Maggie. 1986. *Texas Highways*. July.

Sweet, James. 1972. "The Employment of Rural Farm Wives." *Rural Sociology* 37:553–74.

Taylor, Virginia H. 1976. *Index to Spanish and Mexican Land Grants*. Austin: General Land Office.

Webb, Walter P. 1931. *The Great Plains*. Boston and New York.

Wilkening, Eugene, and Lakshmi K. Bharadwaj. 1967. "Dimensions of Aspirations, Work Roles, and Decision-Making of Farm Husbands and Wives in Wisconsin." *Journal of Marriage and the Family* 29:703–11.

Winegarten, Ruthe. 1985. *Texas Women: A Pictorial History*. Austin: Eakin Press.

Worcester, Don. 1987. *The Texas Longhorn*. College Station: Texas A&M University Press.

Index